QWA QWA
Oxbow
Buthe
UTHA BUTHE
Khubelu
Malibamatso
Senqu
Letseng-la-Terae
Lejone
BE
Matsoku
Moremoholo
Tlokoeng
MOKHOTLONG
Seshote
Mokhotlong
Mokhotlong Airport
Mokhotlong
atse Dam
Senqu
Linakaneng
Linakeng
Linakeng
Thaba
Tseka
Sani Top
Taung
Mashai
Linotsing
Matebeng
Sehlabathebe
Paulus
QACHA'S NEK
Tsoelike
Moshebi
Sekake
Tsoelike
Senqu
Mpiti
Qacha's
Nek
TRANSKEI
N
LESOTHO
CW00460705

VISITORS' GUIDE TO LESOTHO

VISITORS' GUIDE TO LESOTHO

HOW TO GET THERE · WHAT TO SEE · WHERE TO STAY

Marco Turco

SOUTHERN
BOOK PUBLISHERS

This book is fondly dedicated to Jody . . . and with thanks to the trees that gave of themselves to become paper.

ISBN 1 86812 518 1

First edition, first impression 1994

Published by
Southern Book Publishers (Pty) Ltd
PO Box 3103, Halfway House 1685

Cover design by Insight Graphics
Set in 10/11.5 pt Palatino by
Kohler Carton & Print (Natal)
Printed and bound by Kohler Carton & Print (Natal)

ACKNOWLEDGEMENTS

Without the assistance of many people this book would never have reached completion. My sincere thanks go to the following:

To Dr M.L. Mophethe, Mrs Mathe and the staff at the Ministry of Tourism, Sport and Culture in Lesotho.

To Jody Turco and the "babies" who were a constant source of support and encouragement through the weeks of putting all the information together.

To the hoteliers and innkeepers throughout Lesotho, who provided information and moments of relaxation.

To Colin Stevenson for his painful hours of fighting with his graphics program while doing my maps. And to his wife, who had just had a baby, thank you.

To my family and friends who encouraged me to accept the challenge of a book.

To all the Lesotho Government personnel who assisted me in the research – not least Polotso Khali at the Ministry of Information.

To Louise Grantham of Southern Book Publishers, who gave a journalist the opportunity to become a writer.

Finally, to the wonderful people of Lesotho who shared their lives with me, and for a while called me "brother."

CONTENTS

INTRODUCTION

Surrounded by South Africa and hidden between mountain ranges, Lesotho is one of the last "wild" countries left on the African continent. It is not a country for five-star travel, but for those with a sense of adventure and appreciation of nature's splendour, it is undoubtedly a dream destination.

Travelling through Lesotho requires ingenuity, tenacity and an open mind. Towns are far apart, transport is unreliable and the weather unpredictable. But the effort you put in is rewarded by the beauty of the country and hospitality of its people. From the sense of freedom among high wind-swept mountains to the inspiring serenity of tree-filled valleys, from the bustle of district towns to the tranquillity of remote villages, Lesotho has something to excite even the most jaded traveller.

It is impossible to feel indifferent about Lesotho: you cannot avoid being affected by the country and the Basotho. Nothing is ever the way you expect it to be. It becomes what you make of it – the secret is in adjusting your mind, in being receptive, flexible and respectful.

Lesotho cannot be fully appreciated from the confines of a luxury vehicle or the comfort of an airplane, you need to get out and mingle with the blanketed tribesmen, walk along ancient mountain paths and allow your senses to be challenged, assaulted and invigorated. Only in this way will the mystery and intrigue that is Lesotho be unravelled for you.

Like most countries in Africa, Lesotho has its share of political, economic and social turmoil. Visitors should be aware of the complexities of this still predominantly tribal country. While travelling, keep your eyes and ears open for any sudden political changes, and whatever the situation, remain calm and think before speaking. If you follow basic social rules Lesotho will be the vacation of a lifetime. One thing is certain in Lesotho – there is never a dull moment.

This country has a lot to share with the visitor, and even more to teach those who are willing to listen with their soul. But Lesotho is changing: population growth and the demand from agriculture and mining are rapidly destroying the remaining wilderness areas. Around larger towns, once heather-covered hills are now scarred, cultivated terraces. Where remote villages once stood lost in time, now loom the grotesque shapes of heavy mining machinery. Soon, what was once a frontier will be gone. Nevertheless there is no country in Africa that can compare with Lesotho – what it still has to offer is unique. You must go and experience it for yourself.

HOW TO USE THIS GUIDE

Lesotho is not a country that you can visit without prior planning. The first stage is to get a detailed map of Lesotho and contact the nearest Lesotho Tourist Board or embassy for more information about the country. Chapter 1 of this guide is a brief background to Lesotho, while chapter 2 provides facts of relevance to travellers. Next, decide on a route. The three routes detailed in this book are accessible to most 4x4 vehicles, motorbikes and bicycles. Visitors who are uncertain as to how to travel to and within Lesotho should refer to chapters 3 and 4. For budget travellers intending to hike in Lesotho, the priorities are a topographical map, compass, food, water and a strong sense of adventure; introductory information can be found in chapter 7, while further advice can be obtained from the Ministry of Tourism, Sport and Culture. Once you have decided on a route, read the suggested routes in chapter 6. Visitors to Maseru will find pertinent information about the capital in chapter 5. And for those who want to experience the thrill of exploring Lesotho by pony, details are provided in chapter 8.

Once familiar with the theoretical knowledge on Lesotho, you can begin: obtain passports, medical insurance, all the necessary vaccinations, extra passport-size photographs, traveller's cheques or hard cash, and pack your bags!

Take this guide along as a working copy; scribble additional information in the margins, note any changes that may have occurred (as they frequently do in Africa), and then when you return home, write and tell me. All letters received, whether constructive or critical, will be answered and useful information will be filed, to be included in updated editions.

1 FACTS ABOUT THE COUNTRY

HISTORY AND GOVERNMENT

For about 50 000 years before the arrival of the Nguni migration, present-day Lesotho was inhabited by the San people. Considered by many historians to be prehistoric, the San left intricate rock paintings, had a complex social order and a cosmic relationship with the spirit world. In the movement of the negroid tribes from the north, the peace-loving San and much of the wildlife in their territories were eventually wiped out, and have sadly become extinct in Lesotho.

The Basotho had their origins in the low-lying, warm lands of the Tswana tribes in Botswana. Their history, mostly in the form of stories and legends, tells of the journey of the Bakoena tribe from Botswana to Tafelkop in the Orange Free State province of South Africa. Then onto Bethlehem and into the hills around Butha Buthe where they established a settlement on the mountain fortress above the present town. There was however no cohesive peace in the area at that time, and it was left to the foresight of Moshoeshoe the Great to bring a unity and common goal to the warring factions of the region.

Gathering and subjugating tribes he began to mould a nation from those who joined him. Leaving Butha Buthe on 23 June 1824 he trekked, with his people, to Thaba Bosiu and there started fulfilling his dream of a united Basotho people. Soon his well-trained and fierce warriors had extended Moshoeshoe's realm over most of what is now the Orange Free State in South Africa. But as his territory expanded, so Moshoeshoe began to lose control over his more distant chiefs, who frequently decided to take matters into their own hands. The British, ruling South Africa at the time, laid the blame at Moshoeshoe's door and sent a regiment of troops against him at Thaba Bosiu in 1851. They were unable to capture Moshoeshoe and were forced to retreat.

When the British relinquished control over the Orange Free State, they were replaced by the land-grabbing Boers, who viewed the local natives as little more than heathen slaves. Inevitably, they decided to attack Moshoeshoe in his mountain stronghold. Repulsed repeatedly, the Boers continued to wage war against the Basotho from 1865 – 1868 they never managed to conquer Moshoeshoe and his tough Basothos.

Tired of all the fighting and afraid that his fledgling nation might suffer, Moshoeshoe turned to his old enemies for help. He naively asked the British for assistance, with no idea what was about to happen. In 1871 the British Administration, without prior consultation, annexed Lesotho to the Empire. By this time Moshoeshoe's once vast kingdom had shrunk to what is now Lesotho.

To entrench their power further and limit any retaliation, the British issued the Peace Preservation Act in 1880. This Act required that all Basotho turn in their firearms to the nearest British garrison. Not unexpectedly, the Basotho rebelled and there followed nearly four years of fighting in what has become known as the Great Gun War to Basothos, and the Basotho Rebellion to British historians. But Britain never relinquished complete control, and it was possibly just as well. For when, in 1910, South Africa became a self-governing Union, many South African farmers in the Orange Free State began casting covetous glances at Lesotho. Once again Lesotho appealed to the British for help, and the Administration passed a mandate keeping Lesotho a separate colony – meaning that she was a separate country within South Africa.

Finally after years of delicate negotiations the British government granted Lesotho independence on 4 October 1966. King Moshoeshoe II was appointed ruler because of his direct descent from Moshoeshoe the Great.

As time passed, however, two political parties started lobbying for the aristocracy to be replaced by a parliament. Shortly after independence from Britain, the first elections were held in the country; heavily supported by Christian churches, the Basotho National Party, under the leadership of Chief Jonathan, won. Chief Jonathan and King Moshoeshoe II were bitter enemies, and after crushing a dramatic *coup d'état* attempt in 1970, Chief Jonathan turned on the King, who fled to exile in the Netherlands. Becoming increasingly paranoid about his position, Chief Jonathan banned all opposition parties until – in a desperate bid to regain popularity – 1973. Most leaders of the banned political parties remained sceptical of his intentions and refused to join the proposed National Assembly. Chief Jonathan was furious and started a witch-hunt in 1974. Troops and police slaughtered over 400 people and imprisoned many more. Getting worse in his tyrannical control of Lesotho, Chief Jonathan embarked on a series of "purification programmes", supposedly to eradicate the subversive elements in the country. Prominent members of the community began to disappear, and the body of the secretary of the exiled King was found strangled on a deserted country road, as were the mutilated remains of Edgar Mahiba, editor of the *Leselinyana La Lesotho* newspaper. The Basotho people lived in constant fear, and all appeals for help went unheard – that is, until Chief Jonathan provoked the white government in South Africa by openly supporting Frelimo in their fight against the Portuguese in Mozambique and offering safe haven in Lesotho to soldiers of the then banned African National Congress. Soon an ANC base was established from which members would slip into South Africa to wreak mayhem before returning to hide in Lesotho. South Africa retaliated by blockading landlocked Lesotho. Within weeks the country was in grave difficulty: starvation began to claim lives, crime was out of control and Lesotho seemed to be dying. Chief Jonathan, realising his mistake, hurriedly sent a delegation under General Lekhanya to South Africa. Just three days after his secretive talks with the South Africans General Lekhanya, supported by the entire Lesotho armed forces, staged a *coup d'état* which removed Chief Jonathan from power. Within hours of the coup, South African freight vehicles rolled across the border, carrying food, medical supplies and a number of "advisers". All across the world echoed innuendos and suggestions about South Africa's involvement in the coup, but nothing was ever proven.

On 26 March 1993 the first national election in 40 years was held, and saw the Basutoland Congress Party come to power. There is renewed hope in the country: the present leadership actively seeks foreign aid for modernisation and development, and plans to take Lesotho quickly into a democratic First World position.

Although there is no complete history of Lesotho, visitors interested in more detail should consult the following books, recommended by the Lesotho Government's historian:

History of the Basotho, D.F. Ellenberger, Caxton Press, London, 1969.

Moshoeshoe – Chief of the Sotho, P. Sanders, Heineman Educational Books, London, 1975.

Government in Change, L.B.J. Machobane, Macmillan, London, 1990.

GEOGRAPHY AND CLIMATE

The only country in the world with all its territory above 1 000 m, Lesotho is a land of high mountains, deep valleys and cold rivers. It is sparsely populated, and visitors have to rely on their own abilities in remote areas. Surrounded by South Africa along most of its border, Lesotho shares a section of mountains, around Qacha's Nek, with the politically unstable Transkei. Over 75% of Lesotho is highland country, while only 25% in the far western region is considered lowland – anything below 1 800 m is called "lowland". In the east of the country, edging the central Drakensberg, lies the highest peak in southern Africa: Thabana Ntlenyana at 3 483 m.

Lesotho's geographical history is turbulent. With foundations laid an estimated 200 million years ago below sea level, the country is made up of layers of sandstone, brittle shale and mud. Above the compressed mud are palaeolithic Red Beds, a layer of main surface rock and then soft cave sandstone. Millennia of erosion by wind and water whittled away at the sandstone; some of these natural masterpieces can be seen in the western Lesotho lowlands. Then, about 170 million years ago, the entire geography was altered by a series of awesome earthquakes. Molten lava gushed out of fissures and piled up in spongy layers. After the earthquakes, dust storms ceaselessly lashed the land for decades until, once again, lava poured over the shallow valleys from towering volcanoes. And the slow process of erosion began again.

A strange geological feature of Lesotho is that all its rivers flow in the same direction because the lower strata of sandstone were uniformly laid in a north-easterly to south-westerly plan.

Running north-east to south-west the Maluti mountain range dominates the western districts of the country, while the east is made inaccessible by the barrier of the Drakensberg. Lesotho is comprised of 10 districts, whose boundaries follow river courses (see map on endpapers): the Senqunyane river separates the Maseru and Thaba Tseka districts; the Phuthiatsana river the Berea and Leribe districts; Butha Buthe arches across northern Lesotho west of the Matsoku river, east of which lies the remotest of the districts, Mokhotlong. The Senqu river borders Qacha's Nek to the north, Quthing to the south and Mohale's Hoek to the west. The Makhaleng river separates Mohale's Hoek to the east from Mafeteng to the west, and the Tsoaing river borders Mafeteng to the north.

Lesotho is blessed with nearly 300 days a year of glorious sunshine. But even though the sun may warm most days, the night temperature can plummet to below zero even in midsummer. Summer, from November-January, is also the rainy season in Lesotho, and visitors can expect thunder and lightning storms most evenings. Winter is the tourist season in Lesotho, and from May-July hotels and lodges are usually fully booked. Snow covers most of the highland country and many of the remote towns become inaccessible. Skiing is fast becoming a major tourist attraction on Lesotho's mountains and hills. For visitors who travel to experience a country and its people, the best seasons are undoubtedly spring and autumn. Spring lasts from about August-October, autumn from February-April. Visitors arriving during these seasons should head for the isolated mountain villages where ancient African ceremonies are held for the birth of the new earth in spring, or in honour of the ancestors who guide the harvest. These religious observances go unseen by most visitors, and unless you venture off the roads onto the mountain tracks through hidden villages during spring or autumn, you will miss seeing the remnants of a vanishing culture.

FESTIVALS AND HOLIDAYS

Although Christianity is the dominant religion, adhered to by about 75% of the population, other faiths are freely practised, with Islam representing about 3%; there are even smaller minorities of Hindus and Jews. Christianity may be the professed faith of most Basothos, but traditional religious rites such as sun worship, animal and ancestor worship are still observed by most rural clans. Their lives and therefore spiritual faith revolve around the cow. Respectfully titled "God with the wet nose," the cow is used in a number of tribal ceremonies. A person who dies in one of the isolated villages is buried with a cow, which will be the "Great Giver" on the journey to the next phase of existence. Marriage payments are made with cattle, and fines for offences such as theft, adultery or assault are payable only with the best of the offender's cows.

There are 12 recognised holidays in Lesotho. Visitors should note that on these days banks, government offices and most shops are closed.

1 January – New Year's Day
11 March – Moshoeshoe Day
12 March – Colony Day
21 March – Tree Planting Day
Good Friday (date varies)
Easter Monday (date varies)
Ascension Day (date varies)
17 July – King's Birthday
4 October – Independence Day
25 December – Christmas Day
26 December – Family/Boxing Day
Lesotho Sports Day (date varies, but it is always a Monday, usually in the second half of the year)

2 FACTS FOR THE VISITOR

VISAS

Visas are not required by visitors who intend staying less than 30 days in Lesotho. The date of entry and proposed exit date are stamped in your passport when you enter Lesotho. Official passports are required by all visitors, except at the Sani Pass border post, where a South African identity document can be used for a day trip to the Sani Top Chalet and immediate area. The border police keep your identity document until you leave Lesotho.

Should you decide, once already in Lesotho, to stay longer than 30 days, it will be necessary to undergo hours of waiting, reams of paperwork and the patience of Gandhi before an extended visa is issued. The visa is issued free and can take anything from 2–48 hours to process. Sometimes the process can be greatly accelerated by the surreptitious addition – illegal of course – of a few Loti or Rand. It is often less trouble to apply for a visa in South Africa or in another country where Lesotho is represented. In countries where there is no Lesotho representation, a visa can be obtained through the British Embassy. For visitors arriving from destinations in Africa, there are Lesotho diplomatic offices in South Africa (Pretoria), Mozambique (Maputo) and Kenya (Nairobi). Visa applications can also be made directly to the Director of Immigration and Passport Services, P.O. Box 363, Maseru, 100, Lesotho, or from their offices on the corner of Kingsway and Palace road in Maseru. If visiting South Africa, you must have an entry permit and valid visa from the South African authorities.

Documentation about money can become a problem if you intend staying longer than 30 days. When finally leaving the country, you need to produce an Income Tax Clearance Certificate indicating that you were either legally employed in the country, or were self-financed as evidenced by currency exchange receipts from banks. Although these documents are seldom requested, it is worth having them handy at border posts, just in case. One Australian visitor languished in a Mokhotlong jail for over a week – he had neither a valid visa nor bank exchange receipts, and had stayed in Lesotho for over two months before attempting to leave the country via the poorly controlled Sani Pass border post.

CUSTOMS

Visitors to Lesotho are permitted to bring in 1 litre of wine, spirits or any other alcoholic beverage; 400 cigarettes or 50 cigars and up to 300 ml of perfume. However, residents of South Africa, Botswana and Swaziland are not allowed to bring liquor into Lesotho.

Luggage and vehicles are seldom inspected, but in common with customs officials throughout the world, the Lesotho Customs have a knack of selecting a guilty vehicle or person. All visitors arriving with their own transport are required to complete a declaration form stating what they are bringing into Lesotho. A false declaration which doesn't match the contents that are inspected is a guarantee of being shut in a Lesotho prison for at least a few hours and the confiscation of the offending goods.

There are a number of illegal items, and people trying to smuggle them in can expect severe sentences if caught. These include any form of weapon such as bayonets, guns, knives with blades longer than 10 cm and axes. Also, any written or photographic material which is considered politically subversive or pornographic is forbidden. As can be expected, customs officers at the Lesotho, Transkei and South African border posts are particularly strict on anyone found trafficking in drugs. Lesotho grows what is considered some of the best cannabis in the world – most of it entering the market via uncontrolled border areas.

Pets and other animals need special permits to enter or leave Lesotho, as do most plants, seeds and trees. Details can be obtained directly from the Principal Secretary, Ministry of Agriculture, P.O. Box 24, Maseru, 100, Lesotho. Telephone: (International code 09266) 324843.

MONEY

The Loti (M) is divided into 100 lisente (L). There are coins of L50, L25, L10, L5, L2, L1, and notes of M50, M20, M10, M5, M2. The South African Rand is the preferred currency and visitors are able to pay in Rand throughout Lesotho, but do not always expect change in Rand and remember that the Loti is difficult to change outside the country.

You are permitted to bring in unlimited amounts of foreign currency without declaring it. But all transactions involving the cashing of traveller's cheques or changing of foreign currency into Loti should be carried out in the capital, Maseru.

Very few of the banks in Maseru will issue a receipt with the transaction statement, and some bank clerks don't even know what a receipt is! However, for visitors intending to stay longer than 30 days in Lesotho it is important to insist on and keep receipts. The reason is that when you apply for an Income Tax Clearance Certificate, for a stay of longer than 30 days, the civil servants issuing the certificate are required to see proof of all monetary transactions which indicate that you have been supporting yourself and not earning money illegally in Lesotho.

In Maseru you can change most foreign currencies and traveller's cheques, but in rural areas foreign currency, except for the South African Rand, is useless – even at hotels and lodges. Do not expect the latest exchange rates at the banks and be prepared for a wait while clerks phone the banks across the border for monetary values on your particular currency. It is best to stick to pound sterling or US dollars in foreign exchange and keep the denominations fairly large because you want to change money as infrequently as possible. Some hotels, called "International," will cash traveller's cheques, but at a reduced rate.

Few places outside Maseru accept credit cards, and those that do charge exorbitant handling fees. A better idea is to do your major currency exchanges into Rand across the border in South Africa, and use Rands for all payments in Lesotho. If you do decide to change money in Lesotho make sure that the money you are given is in adequately small denominations. There seems to be a constant lack of small change in the country and if you let vendors keep the extra money it can quite soon add up to a considerable amount. Never accept any torn or dirty notes – they are always difficult to get rid of.

A higher exchange rate can be had on the black market, which operates quite openly but is illegal.

There is no ideal way of carrying money while travelling, but using a moneypouch or moneybag is better than wallets and handbags. Split your money up: carry some on your person, leave some in your vehicle or backpack and some at the hotel when you stroll around the town or village. To keep the money from getting damp and tatty while you are carrying it, put the notes into a plastic zip-lock packet inside the pouch.

If you intend taking money out of Lesotho by converting back to your original currency, the bank changing the money will endorse your passport and will not permit you to change more than M500 at a time.

Banking hours in urban centres:
Monday, Tuesday, Thursday and Friday 08h30–15h30
Wednesday 08h30–13h00
Saturday 08h30–11h00.

COSTS

A number of factors make accurate forecasts of costs in Lesotho difficult. The finances for each trip need to be calculated – remember that the budget must be flexible and sufficient to cover any unexpected emergencies. Ask yourself questions such as, What standard of accommodation am I prepared to pay for (when there is a choice)? How much am I expecting to spend on curios and other Basotho goods? Will I be using my own transport, public transport or hitchhiking?

A rough estimate is that a budget of about M150 per adult a day in the larger towns and M50 in the village areas will cover accommodation, meals and guides. This excludes the price of fuel, which can be as high as M2.50 per litre at remote places such as Oxbow. Public transport is relatively cheap and the average price for a 60 km bus or minibus taxi journey is M10. If you are hitching, do not be surprised when the driver expects some payment. Rather ask before accepting a lift. If you spend most of your time in the rural areas, your costs will be very low and you may well find yourself returning home with money. But in larger towns the price of most things is high.

DOCUMENTS

A passport is required from all visitors entering Lesotho – the only exception is at the Sani Pass border post (see Northern Route). If you are entering from any country north of South Africa, a valid International Vaccination Card is also required, especially from countries where yellow fever or cholera is endemic. It is important that the expiry date in your passport covers the period you intend staying in Lesotho. For safety, it is usually a good idea to make photocopies of the first two or three pages of your passport and keep them in a separate place from the original (do this also for traveller's cheques.)

Visitors arriving with their own transport, specifically from beyond southern Africa, will need an International Certificate of Motor Vehicles (this is your vehicle's personal passport) and an International Driving Permit, either in English or a certified translation, which is accepted in Lesotho for a maximum period of six months. These permits are issued by most motoring organisations to valid licence holders over the age of 18, and can also be used when you apply to rent a vehicle. Vehicle insurance, though seldom asked for, is important for any trip to Lesotho. Vehicles arriving from north of South Africa require a fully paid Carnet de Passages en Douanes. This document enables you to import your vehicle temporarily and prevents your selling it in Lesotho without paying the necessary import tax. The document, issued by motoring organisations, requires that you deposit the value of your vehicle with them – the deposit is returned when you hand in your Carnet. Nationality plates are seldom checked, but just to be on the safe side it is better to affix them. Proof of ownership of the vehicle is required and consists of receipts from the purchase of the vehicle and the road licence from the issuing authority.

Another document that visitors from outside the South African Customs Area might consider is an International Camping Carnet. This is issued by the International Automobile Federation. While the International Camping Carnet serves little purpose within Lesotho - there are virtually no official campsites - it does serve as a suitable character reference from an international organisation. This character reference is necessary should you wish to get a press card or official letter of introduction from the Ministry of Tourism to remote regions of the country. For visitors overlanding across Africa, the International Camping Carnet serves the same purpose as the Carnet de Passages en Douanes; it is your camping passport and verification that you will not try and sell your equipment while travelling through the country. If you plan to take a large amount of expensive photographic equipment into Lesotho it is advisable to bring all receipts of purchase from your home country. A journalist from Sweden was recently forced to pay export tax on his camera equipment because he was unable to furnish proof of purchase.

Lesotho is one of the few countries in the world where an International Student Identity Card is still useful. Concessions for holders of these cards include airline tickets, long-distance bus fares and even some hotels in the larger towns. The International Youth Hostel Federation Card will ensure a reduction in the price of staying at the few youth hostels in the country. Fakes of these cards are for sale in South Africa, Botswana and Zimbabwe; using them is of course fraudulent.

TIPPING

Salaries in Lesotho are abominably low, even compared to those in other Third World countries. In many occupations, tips make the difference between a simple meal and hunger. Tips are also often the best way of "smoothing" your visit: a table in a full restaurant, an extra seat in a packed bus or the quick processing of a visa.

Be wary though, there is a difference between giving to beggars and tipping your waiter at the hotel. The rules of "compassionate charity" or "getting things done" should be observed before you part with your money. Western customs of tipping 10–15% of the meal bill do not apply in Lesotho; a few lisente will suffice.

CONSULATES AND EMBASSIES

The few countries with consular representatives in Lesotho have their offices in Maseru, the capital. Countries that have diplomatic offices in Lesotho are:

Denmark

Address: (Postal): P.O. Box 1259, Maseru
(Physical): Site 16, Industrial Reserve, Maseru
Telephone: 323630

France

Address: (Postal): Private Bag A191, Maseru
(Physical): 37 Qoaling Road, Maseru
Telephone: 326050

Germany

Address: (Postal and physical): 10th Floor, Lesotho Bank Building, Maseru
Telephone: 312750

Great Britain

Address: (Postal): P.O. Box 521, Maseru
(Physical): Linare Road, Central, Maseru
Telephone: 313961

Ireland

Address: (Postal): Private Bag A67, Maseru
(Physical): 2nd Floor, Christie House, Maseru
Telephone: 314068

Netherlands

Address: (Postal): P.O. Box 288, Maseru
Telephone: 312269

South Africa

Address: (Postal): Private Bag A266, Maseru
(Physical): 1st Floor, Lesotho Bank Building, Maseru
Telephone: 325758

Sweden

Address: (Postal): Private Bag A175, Maseru
(Physical): 1st Floor, Lesotho Bank Building, Maseru
Telephone: 311555

Switzerland

Address: (Postal): P.O. Box 708, Maseru
Telephone: 311585

United States of America

Address: (Postal): P.O. Box 333, Maseru
(Physical): Kingsway Road, Maseru
Telephone: 312666/7

LESOTHO DIPLOMATIC MISSIONS ABROAD

Belgium

Embassy of the Kingdom of Lesotho
Address: 66 Cortenberch Boite, 5, 1040, Brussels
Telephone: 7363976/7

Canada

High Commission of the Kingdom of Lesotho
Address: 22 Clemow Avenue, Ottawa, Ontario, Kis 2B4
Telephone: (613) 2369449

Denmark

Embassy of the Kingdom of Lesotho
Address: Osterkildevej 14, DK–2820, Gentofte
Telephone: (31) 651442

Germany

Embassy of the Kingdom of Lesotho
Address: Godesberger Alle 50, 5300, Bonn, 2
Telephone: (228) 376868/9

Great Britain

High Commission of the Kingdom of Lesotho
Address: 10 Collingham Road, London, SW5 0NR
Telephone: (0047) 3738581/2

Italy

Embassy of the Kingdom of Lesotho
Address: Via Di Porta Pertusa, 4, Rome–00165
Telephone: (6) 6378183

Kenya

High Commission of the Kingdom of Lesotho
Address: International Life House, Mama Ngina Street, Nairobi
Telephone: 224876

Mozambique

Embassy of the Kingdom of Lesotho
Address: Ave Kim Il Sung 1138, Maputo
Telephone: 490959

United States of America

Embassy of the Kingdom of Lesotho
Address: 2511 Massachussetts Avenue, N.W., Washington DC, 20008
Telephone: (202) 797533/4/5/6

TOURIST INFORMATION

The Lesotho Government has established several offices where brochures, maps and pertinent information can be obtained. Lesotho is part of the Southern African Regional Tourism Council (SARTOC), and the headquarters of Lesotho Tourism are in Malawi.

Postal address: SARTOC, P.O. Box 564, Blantyre, Malawi
Telephone: (09265) 634888

The information from SARTOC is however limited and visitors will find the Lesotho Tourist Office in Maseru a lot more helpful.

Postal address: Lesotho Tourist Board, P.O. Box 1378, Maseru 100
Physical address: Victoria Hotel Building, 209 Kingsway Road, Maseru
Telephone: (09266) 322892 or 323760

Visitors from South Africa who are interested in obtaining information about Lesotho before arriving in the country should contact the Lesotho Information Office.

Address: Lesotho Tourism Board, 132 Jan Smuts Ave, Parkwood, Johannesburg P.O. Box 600, Parklands 2121
Telephone: (011) 7880742

OR

Address: Lesotho Trade Mission, Indent House, President Street, Johannesburg
Telephone: (011) 290751

Lesotho has no specific tourist information centres in other countries, but tourists can obtain information about Lesotho either directly from the Tourist Board in Lesotho or from any Embassy of the Kingdom of Lesotho (see previous section). Bear in mind that the information supplied through overseas Diplomatic Missions is often outdated and should be used more as a planning guide than a travel guide.

Postal services

The main GPO in Maseru is the most efficient and reliable post office in which to do any postal business. Maseru has a workable poste restante system, and people expecting mail should ask for the Postmaster who will give you a box of unfiled letters. If you want someone from outside Lesotho to write to you, the procedure is straightforward: your surname should precede your (passport) names on the envelope, followed by c/o Poste Restante, Maseru Post Office, Maseru 100, Lesotho. The letters will be kept for three months, then placed in "File 13" which is simply the fire. When sending letters or parcels from Lesotho make sure the stamps are franked in front of you, there have been occasions when letters and parcels have arrived at their destinations without stamps but with a covering charge from the local post office.

It is far more reliable to travel to Maseru for posting and receiving letters, as the post is frequently delayed in reaching the more distant post offices. Airplanes usually deliver post, but with the unpredictable and often severe weather conditions common to Lesotho, the arrival of the postal plane is uncertain.

Telex

Only the main GPO in Maseru has telex facilities, but you'll need a Press Card from the Ministry of Information before you are allowed to use them. Money orders can be telexed to Maseru. If you are expecting a money order, put aside at least five hours for the process, and have your passport available for inspection.

Time

The same as in South Africa: Greenwich Mean Time plus 2 hours all year round.

Telephone

Lesotho has a telephone system that is good in Maseru and gets worse the further east you travel. International telephone calls are supposedly possible from all destinations in Lesotho, but to be sure of making the connection it is better to do your international phoning from Maseru or one of the larger urban centres, which are located mostly on the western side of the country. From these centres the calls are put through relatively quickly, and there is the advantage of being able to pre-book calls and then continue seeing the town until the appointed time. Beware of making international calls from hotel rooms; the hotels all charge extremely high handling fees and often listen in on conversations.

Business hours

Business and shopping hours are the same: 08h00 to 17h00 weekdays and 08h00 to 13h00 on Saturdays. Civil Service departments have slightly different working times: 08h00 to 16h30, but closed from 12h45 to 14h00 for lunch. Banks are open only from 8h30 to 13h00 weekdays and 8h30 to 11h00 on Saturdays. The best time to change currency or cash traveller's cheques is between 9h00 and 10h00 on weekdays. At this time banks are relatively empty and the service is good. Forget Saturdays and either side of a public holiday.

Official hours of business do not apply to street vendors, village stores and eating or drinking establishments, the latter usually being open for at least 18 hours per day.

Electricity is not available everywhere in Lesotho, and although monster-like high voltage lines criss-cross the whole country, large areas are still without electricity and rely on candles or diesel-powered generators. This is inevitably the crazy irony of Third World countries and Lesotho, unfortunately, is no different. It is therefore advisable to carry a torch, spare batteries, matches or lighter and a few candles.

MEDIA

There are two national newspapers in Lesotho, one in English and the other in Sesotho; both are weekly publications. Newspapers from South Africa are delivered daily and cover all major world events.

Magazines and books are available in the larger towns from shops such as the CNA in Kingsway Road, a block north of the Tourist Office. Unlike travelling through other African countries, there are few long or boring journeys in Lesotho, and the sight of a traveller sitting on the bus reading a book is uncommon.

Lesotho does have television with one local network in collaboration with South Africa's M-Net Network. Programmes are also broadcast from South Africa on SABC TV channels or on channel television, M-Net. Most hotels and lodges have television – some of the better, in each room – but because the reception is often poor, VCRs and videos have become increasingly popular. Radio stations within Lesotho are under the direct control of the state, but virtually all localities are able to receive a variety of programmes from South African stations.

SPORTS

The Basotho are a sport-orientated nation. Soccer, the national sport, is followed with great gusto, from the modern stadiums in the towns to the sloping fields high in the mountains. Crowds of people gather for these games and it is worthwhile attending a match and letting yourself get caught up in the excitement. The times and dates of major soccer matches can be obtained from the Lesotho Sports Council in Maseru.

Postal address: Lesotho Sports Council, P.O. Box 138, Maseru 100
Telephone: (09266) 323734

HEALTH

As when visiting most African countries, you need to be fit and healthy before attempting Lesotho. Though free, thanks to its altitude, of the more common African ailments such as yellow fever, bilharzia and malaria, Lesotho does present certain medical problems for visitors. Prepare yourself with as much emergency medical knowledge as possible; a useful book to read is *Where There Is No Doctor*, written by D. Werner and published by Macmillan Press, London. AIDS has become endemic to most African countries, and Lesotho is no exception. When packing your first-aid kit, include your own sealed hypodermics and a stamped doctor's prescription for any scheduled drugs you need.

Before entering Lesotho, be sure to take all the required vaccinations: yellow fever, cholera and polio, and for added safety tetanus, tuberculosis, gamma globulin for infectious hepatitis A and a course of tablets for typhoid fever (trade name: Vivotif Berna). It takes considerable time to have all these treatments and you should start at least six weeks before your departure. Contact your local government health department to have the yellow fever, cholera and polio vaccinations.

It is important that people touring Lesotho take out some form of medical insurance. The insurance must cover any illness, the cost of medical treatment and prescribed medication. Medical treatment for foreigners in Lesotho is expensive and of poor quality, so many ill travellers head for South Africa and its cheaper but better medical services. Ask any travel agent about the options and companies that deal with medical health insurance.

Do not drink any naturally occurring water in Lesotho; though the elevation is high enough to prevent bilharzia in the water, other diseases can be picked up. Two of the more nasty ones are hepatitis and dysentery. The locals seem to have little trouble with drinking the water, but Western stomachs often cannot handle the invasion. Be careful, too, of fruit and vegetables that have been washed in unboiled water. Carry your own waterbottle, which you can replenish at hotels, and a supply of water-purification tablets or iodine drops.

Diarrhoea can be a problem if you are not careful of what you eat. Much of the Basotho food is mainly starch and lacks vitamins and elements. A good defence is to take along a supply of multivitamin tablets and fortified dehydrated drinks such as Complan. Travelling through Lesotho is demanding, and many people find themselves sweating more than usual; it is vital that your body salts be replaced if you are to avoid getting cramped muscles and losing strength. Include salt in at least one meal per day to keep body salt levels replenished.

Teeth must also be attended to prior to your visiting Lesotho. The towns are far apart and the roads often terrible, which makes covering any distance with toothache a painful experience. Go to your dentist for a check-up and any medical treatment you may need at least four weeks before departure. Though unpleasant, a short-term solution to toothache if you are far from treatment is to pour a little Oil of Cloves onto cottonwool and press it against the offending tooth.

Sunburn is common among travellers to Lesotho. Many think that because of the altitude they won't burn, but with the clear mountain air and strong reflections some degree of sunburn is inevitable, especially between the hours of 11h00 and 14h00. Take along a sun-protection cream of at least a factor 5 strength and apply it to the exposed areas of the skin before going outside.

Visitors who wear glasses should take along either an extra pair or a prescription for a new pair. In Maseru prescription glasses can be made at: Optica (Pty) Ltd, Nkhatho Building, Corner Parliament and Airport Street, Maseru. Tel. 311285.

Hepatitis

This disease entails a viral attack on the liver, and if you contract hepatitis it will probably be of the type A. To avoid hepatitis keep everything as clean as possible – a difficult thing to do in Lesotho. Drink only purified or boiled water, be careful of meat dishes from street vendors and wash your hands before eating.

The virulent form of hepatitis type B is contracted only from using infected needles or having sex with a carrier. If you think you might have a sexual encounter while in Lesotho make certain to include some form of protection against sexual infection, for example condoms, and use them or insist that your partner does. (For additional forms of protection, contact your doctor or local health clinic before leaving for Lesotho.)

There is no guaranteed cure for hepatitis and an infected person will need rest and expensive medical treatment. It makes good sense therefore to be immunised before leaving home. Symptoms usually appear about 20–30 days after contact; there is a rapid rise in temperature, loss of appetite, weakness in the limbs and pain below the ribs. White skin and white of the eyes turn a pale yellowish colour and urine changes to a light red. Seek immediate medical attention; if you are still in Lesotho cancel the rest of your trip and get to a hospital in South Africa as quickly as possible.

Typhoid

Typhoid is contracted from contaminated food and water. Visitors must be careful when eating or drinking anywhere in Lesotho.

Diarrhoea

Among visitors who stay longer than 30 days in Lesotho it will be extremely rare to find one who has not succumbed to diarrhoea at least once. Hygiene is not of the highest standard in Lesotho; there are flies everywhere and it is their habits that usually cause infected food to be eaten. Try to eat only freshly cooked food and drink only purified water.

The best solution when you develop diarrhoea is to try your own remedies, which means that initially you should do: nothing. Do not eat for a day or so, but keep body fluids up by drinking lots of liquid, notably tea and a meat-stock drink. Avoid travelling and get lots of rest. Within a day or two the diarrhoea should have cleared itself up. If not, take Lomotil and eat only dry foods, but keep drinking liquid. In the larger towns, visit a pharmacist who will usually prescribe a course of broad-spectrum antibiotics.

Dysentery

This problem is more serious than normal diarrhoea and is marked by mucus and blood in your stools. Bacillary dysentery is fairly common, easily cured and does not last very long. Amoebic dysentery on the other hand can cause permanent damage to the large intestine and must be treated immediately. The symptoms are severe stomach cramps, nausea and a high fever, followed by frequent bowel movements and a feeling of weakness. Infected people must get to a medical facility quickly, where strong antibiotics are given and the patient is required to rest and eat healthy food.

Venereal disease (including AIDS)

Gonorrhoea is prevalent in Lesotho and AIDS is quickly becoming a problem. The largest infected group is the miners who travel between their rural homes and the cities of South Africa. But with the recent increase in tourism, a thriving prostitution racket has grown, especially at the larger tourist-orientated hotels. Be aware of the dangers, use condoms and take the necessary precautions during sexual contact. The obvious solution is still abstinence.

Finally, don't worry unduly about your health while in Lesotho. Few visitors are ever seriously affected by any illness, and apart from the odd stomach upset, people usually return home healthier and more invigorated than when they left.

CLOTHING

Lesotho is a country of extremes, and the temperature can range from 30 °C during the day to below zero at night. In summer light clothing can be worn but a jersey is recommended for the evenings. Rain-gear should be taken along throughout the year. Winter brings snowfalls, storms and icy winds. Whatever clothes you decide to take, make sure that they are of natural fibres which allow your skin to breathe while at the same time providing protection from the elements. Make a list of clothing when you plan your trip, aiming to keep your luggage as light as possible.

Summer days are long and warm, and most visitors will find shorts and T-shirts suitable. A guide of what to take in summer could look something like this:

1 pair long trousers
2 T-shirts
3 sets underwear
1 light jersey
1 pair plastic sandals
1 pair town shoes
1 sunhat
1 wind cheater
2 pairs shorts/skirts
1 sweatshirt
4 pairs socks
rain-gear
1 pair hiking boots
1 swimming costume
1 towel
sunglasses

Whatever your choice of clothing, remember that modesty is highly regarded in Lesotho, especially in the rural village areas. Men should avoid walking around without shirts on, and women should not wear short shorts or miniskirts.

Winter requires a great deal more clothing, particularly if you intend visiting the mountain regions. Although there is no need for specialised clothing, adequate protection against the cold is important. To the above list for summer add:

1 heavy jacket	1 blanket shirt
Set of thermal underwear	1 pair corduroy or flannel trousers
2 pairs thick woollen socks	1 pair gloves
1 scarf	1 woollen hat

Clothing must be comfortable; anything that restricts movement will become a nightmare on those arduous journeys. A traditional Basotho blanket is a useful addition to your list: it can be used for sitting on, lying on, sleeping under and huddling into. These blankets are cheap and available at even the most remote stores.

WOMEN VISITORS

Compared to some other African countries, Lesotho is safe for women travellers. Understand, though, that as is typical in rural African communities, women are not held in high regard and in isolated villages are considered less important than cattle. Women tourists are however viewed in a different manner and respect can be expected. Care must however still be taken, primarily in the shanty areas of larger towns.

Avoid walking alone at night, especially through poorly lit alleys and sidestreets. One area from which bad reports have been received is the market square, near Our Lady of Victories Cathedral in Maseru. Several women volunteer workers have been bothered there, mostly on Friday and Saturday nights. On buses, try to find a seat either with another woman or with tourists. This usually discourages the advances of inebriated miners returning home from months away in South Africa.

Clothing also goes a long way towards keeping your journey through Lesotho pleasant. While Basotho women are allowed to expose their breasts even in public areas, the same liberty does not extend to tourists, and you are guaranteed to get arrested if you try and do the same. While ethnic dress is almost *de rigueur* among the volunteer workers in Lesotho, the Basotho people do not consider this suitable for foreigners. Very short skirts or shorts are frowned upon, and if you insist on wearing these you will be hassled by older youths and men. The same is true for "see-through" clothing.

Take all your own feminine hygiene products to Lesotho. There is very limited stock available and even that is marked at a ludicrously high price. When visiting remote villages, women travellers must get used to being stared at, particularly by the young women. Remember that your actions will have an effect on their view of other travellers – try to answer their questions, no matter how personal they might seem.

Avoid the obvious mistakes, such as accepting a lift in a vehicle with only male passengers. Refuse invitations into drinking establishments where there are only men. Pay attention to your code of dress, keeping modesty in mind.

Though very few women travel alone in Lesotho, those who do usually have high praise for the manners of the people. With a little common sense and respect for local customs, there should be no difference between a male or female visiting Lesotho unescorted.

PHOTOGRAPHY

The Basotho have a paranoia about photography. With a legacy of *coup d'états*, infiltration by the South African military and a tense peace with neighbouring Transkei, their fears are well founded. With a strange mixture of Christian and Shamanic beliefs many Basotho are averse to having their picture taken. Always ask before taking a photo of someone. In areas popular with tourists you can expect to have to negotiate a fee before taking the photo. In other areas, common courtesy must be practised. Many visitors are offended when asked for money for taking photographs, but picture the image you present to these people: you arrive with expensive cameras, proper clothing and, often, top of the range offroad vehicles. Ask yourself the question: Who is really being used?

Good quality film is available in Maseru, but film on sale in the other towns is usually old and not recommended. There is no limit to the number of rolls of film or amount of camera equipment you may take into Lesotho. Try to bring all your own photographic requirements, especially film. What could be worse than running out of film as the snow starts to fall, gently draping stone villages and blanketing the surrounding peaks? There are literally thousands of opportunities for photographers. The clear air in the higher regions results in sharp, strong images, a factor that needs to be considered if photos are not to be overexposed.

NEVER take photos of anything that could be considered a military target; these include RLMP (police) stations, border posts, bridges, military barracks, banks, post offices, airports and the Katse Dam Highlands Water Scheme Project. If you are caught, all your equipment will be confiscated, you'll be fined and imprisoned, and your embassy will find it extremely difficult getting a "spy" released.

With the number of opportunities available, visitors should try to take along a good camera, three lenses (28 mm, 30–80 mm, 70–200 mm), spare batteries, lots of colour film, a blue and orange filter, a polariser filter and a cleaning kit. Though this equipment will provide for superb photos, a standard 35 mm camera will also take good "snap-shots".

SECURITY

Theft is not a major problem in Lesotho: the Basotho people are renowned for their scrupulous honesty. But, as in all countries, there are bad elements. Keep your valuable documents with you at all times. At hotels and lodges make sure that your room door is securely locked and any valuable possessions are either hidden away or handed in at the reception desk.

When walking through the streets, avoid obvious displays of wealth, such as conspicuous watches, wads of money or lots of jewellery. Many local people live in abject poverty and the sight of all this accessible wealth can be a great temptation. In the unlikely event of being robbed, never retaliate, rather give them what they demand and immediately report the matter to the Royal Lesotho Mounted Police (RLMP). When camping near a town, watch your possessions. Crowds of children frequently appear as soon as you begin to set up camp, and if you are careless, items could go missing. In the more isolated areas theft is unheard of, and when you visit a village it is quite likely that the headman will assign a youngster to guard your belongings.

If you are sleeping on a bus or minibus taxi at night, secure your luggage to the seat or to a convenient pole with a combination lock and chain. Visitors with their own transport should avoid parking in dark alleys or far from their hotel. At camp, tie a length of chain from your vehicle to your tent guy-ropes as an alarm, should someone try to steal your vehicle. Even inside the tent, simple security rules should be followed, such as putting your valuables at the bottom of your sleeping bag, or between you and the other person. Do not leave anything lying around, especially if a crowd has gathered. Carry money and essential documents in a chest or waist pouch, and hang cameras around your neck rather than shoulder. Buy small padlocks for your luggage or backpacks and either lock the zips together or sew canvas strips with eyelets onto the side of the bags and lock these to zips.

Sadly, there have been increasing reports of visitors having their things stolen by other travellers. The luggage room at the Maseru Tourist Office, where travellers can leave their packs or bags while visiting the city, has a particularly bad reputation. Take out travel insurance that adequately covers your possessions – although this will be little compensation when your rolls of exposed film are stolen. Just be sensible in what you do and the chances of having anything stolen while in Lesotho are rare.

PLACES TO STAY

Tourists used to 5-star accommodation and service will be hard pressed to find anything suitable outside Maseru. For the adventurer and the visitor who has come to see the wilderness and meet the people, there is a wide variety of places to stay and the hospitality of the Basotho is legendary.

The only First-World standard hotels are found in Maseru. These have swimming pools, room and laundry service and restaurants. One of the major drawbacks of these hotels is the high tariff they charge, and there are often extra costs that appear on your bill.

Outside Maseru there are youth hostels, inns, tourist lodges, small hotels, agricultural training centres and one-room shacks. Missions also accommodate travellers, and though they cannot always provide a room and meal, camping is always possible. (Remember to leave a suitable donation when departing.) In the villages, do not expect to find any purpose built tourist accommodation; the corner of a stone hut on an earthen floor is all you are likely to get. This in itself is worth experiencing: with the fire casting shadows on the thatched roof and the wind howling outside the open door, carrying with it the whispers of Africa's space, the smell of milk and visions of the pensive faces of quiet shepherds – it is like living in a Rider Haggard novel.

In the larger towns there is usually an hotel or inn available to visitors. There does not seem to be a standard price for hotels in Lesotho, but you can expect to pay a high price for a bed. It is often a good idea to try the suburbs on the edges of town where it is relatively easy to find a cheap meal and bed for the night. Look for the painted tin signs hanging above doorways. Another place to find accommodation in towns is at the Agricultural Training Centres. These consist of barracks-style accommodation, provided for agricultural students and staff. Over weekends and during vacation time the centres are empty and bunk beds, showers and kitchen facilities become open to visitors at a reasonable price. Contact the matron of the centre who will tell you whether room is available.

Official campsites are nonexistent in Lesotho, but with so much open land and a sparse population, people arriving with their own tents will have no trouble finding a pitch. It is considered good manners to ask the local chief for permission before pitching your tent. If you arrive in a town late at night and find no accommodation, the RLMP (police) will allow you to sleep in a cell for the night – and will even quite happily lock you in!

Availability of accommodation in Lesotho is not a problem, but trying to find it can be. While the larger hotels and tourist lodges are well signposted, the smaller places are not. As very few towns have street-lighting, try to arrive before sunset. Ask at the eating houses or shops where accommodation can be found, or simply set off among the houses until someone points out a place. Avoid camping too near towns, and rather walk out for an hour or so before pitching your tent. A place to stay can always be found in Lesotho, and after overcoming the culture shock, visitors will find themselves worrying less and less about finding a bed.

FOOD

Hygiene is poor and many visitors find themselves eating mainly vegetarian meals. Street vendors offer a variety of good quality vegetables and fruit, but be careful of goods washed in unpurified water: always wash produce thoroughly in pure water before eating it. If heading for the remote regions of Lesotho stock up with vegetables and fruit before leaving. It makes a useful gift in the villages where you may be invited to stay or share a meal.

Maize or sorghum porridge is the basis of most Basotho meals. In the northern areas of the country around Mokhotlong, the street vendors bake a heavy brown bread that is both delicious and nutritious. It maintains its freshness well and can make an interesting change from canned or dehydrated food. Another tasty dish sold by street vendors is mutton stew in a hot peppery sauce – use slices of stiff porridge to mop up the sauce and stringy pieces of mutton. Corn on the cob roasted over a fire is another speciality of the street markets; it makes a wonderful snack while one explores the town.

Almost all trading stores stock a few tins of food, the usual being pilchards in tomato sauce, curried vegetables and corned meat. In the high mountain areas Basotho meals consist of nothing more than a type of gruel mixed with goat or sheep milk. Slightly bitter, the porridge is filling and unlike anything most visitors have ever tasted. Feel free to offer these people some of your provisions: any offer of a change in diet is well received.

Do not expect to get fat in Lesotho, but the opportunity to eat some of the tribal meals should not be missed. It is considered an honour to have a visitor for a meal and travellers should politely accept such an invitation; after all, the meal offered can hardly be spared.

If you feel compelled to give to beggars, give some sort of food rather than money – it may not be well received, but the significance is clear in all cultures.

If you have spent time in the wilderness areas, take advantage of the menus available in larger towns. A good meal does wonders for your health and frame of mind.

Alcohol is freely available and cheap in Lesotho. Most of the canned and bottled beer is made under licence from the multinational South African Breweries; it is of good quality and has a high alcohol content. Alcohol abuse is a problem in Lesotho, and many visitors are amazed at the number of drunks around. The reasons for the high incidence of alcoholism have not yet been fully researched but experienced travellers, who have visited other Third-World countries, will quickly figure out probable causes. This "westernised" beer can be bought from bottle-stores, street vendors and at any of the numerous drinking houses scattered through towns and larger villages. Hotels, of course, have well stocked bars and extensive wine lists. For a taste of the traditional Basotho beer, look for a white flag on a long pole. This is a sign that cereal beer has recently been brewed and is available. Drinking this beer takes a little getting used to, because it bears absolutely no resemblance to western beer. The technique adopted by most visitors is to try to sip the thick liquid; this just draws the agony out. Rather, take one of the plastic 1 litre containers offered to you, stop breathing and take a large gulp. First, your taste buds will riot, then your brain sends warning messages and finally you swallow. By the time you have courageously finished half the container the beer begins to taste quite good, and by the end you won't care what it tastes like.

Food and drink in Lesotho will only present a problem to those with very weak stomachs. Not always of the highest standard, the food satisfies most hunger, is simple and often bland but always an experience. You will soon find that the setting makes the difference, more than the meal; from Mokhotlong brown bread and tomato at the top of the Tlaeeng Pass (3 275 m) to grilled sirloin steak in the Maseru Sun hotel, even eating in Lesotho is part of the adventure.

BOOKS

There are not many books available that offer information about Lesotho, but those that are, are well worth reading:

- *South Africa, Lesotho, Swaziland* by Lonely Planet Guide Books (Lonely Planet Publications, Victoria, Australia)

  This book gives a brief description of Lesotho and some of the main towns. It is aimed primarily at the independent traveller using public transport or hitching, but there is a small section on travelling with your own transport.
- *Lesotho* by David Ambrose (Winchester Press, Maseru, Lesotho)

  This is one of the few guide books devoted exclusively to Lesotho. Although a little dated, it still has loads of useful advice for visitors. It also contains maps and excursion routes, all accompanied by photographs. It can be found in most South African libraries or bought from the Tourist Office in Maseru. For a general introduction to the Basotho people and their country this book makes for good pre-trip reading.
- *Mountains of Southern Africa* by David Bristow (Struik Publishers, Cape Town, South Africa)

  For hikers and climbers this book provides the ideal primer to the mountains of Lesotho. It includes sections on the flora and fauna, the development of the mountains, the tribal populations and a fascinating section on the history of climbing in the Drakensberg.
- *Southern Africa, Land of Beauty and Splendour* by T.V. Bulpin (Reader's Digest, Cape Town, South Africa)

  A well illustrated large format book with a wealth of information for prospective travellers. Giving brief descriptions of most countries in southern Africa, the book includes a few pages on Lesotho supported by stunning photography.

Choose just one or two books to take along on the trip; books are heavy and take up valuable space in a backpack or bag. Books for light reading are uncommon in Lesotho and you will be hard pressed to find any reading material outside the towns. In any case, there is usually not enough time to sit back and read while visiting Lesotho; the scenery is impressive and the people are talkative.

MAPS

The most useful maps of Lesotho are those from the Lesotho Tourist Board and the Automobile Association. These maps should be studied before you arrive in Lesotho, and visitors with their own transport should take note where roads start and end. Because of the many hills and valleys there are areas in Lesotho where no roads exist, the villages being supplied by air.

The colourful map from the Lesotho Tourist Board is 1:714 000 scale, and has a useful street plan of Maseru on the back. Far better is the 1:785 000 AA map. This map includes valuable information, from touring formalities to youth accommodation. It features similar things to the Tourist Board map and includes a larger area of South Africa – useful to South African visitors. The major difference between the two maps is that the Tourist Board map includes recently tarred roads and is more colourful, but leaves out certain places of interest and tourist accommodation. The AA map, coloured in a dull beige and brown, includes more hotels, lodges and inns, plus spot heights, accurate distances, airports, pass heights and road indicators.

Hikers and climbers should try to obtain detailed topographical maps of the area they intend visiting, from the Geological Survey in Lesotho: Department of Geological Survey, P.O. Box 876, Maseru, 100, Lesotho.

THINGS TO BUY

Lesotho offers shoppers a multitude of opportunities for spending money. While in the tourist shops of downtown Maseru the prices are high and fixed, on the streets and in the villages bargaining is expected behaviour. Avoid the stalls and shops in the larger towns mostly frequented by tourists and rather go curio hunting in the mountain villages or from street vendors in the sidestreets.

Lesotho is famous for its mohair and woollen products, especially jerseys, rugs and shawls. In many settlements craft centres have been set up by aid organisations; they operate on a co-operative system. In the villages raw untreated woollen jerseys and blankets can be bought from the women who knit them through the bitter months of winter. These jerseys and blankets are scratchy and dull in colour, but their ability to keep out the elements, even rain, is unsurpassed by any machine-knitted product. More comfortable and colourfully designed jerseys, scarves and shawls can be found in the larger towns, in places such as Lesotho Knits in the centre of Maputsoe, Butha Buthe Woollen Factory in Butha Buthe and the Mohair Cottage in the Maseru Sun Cabanas.

Sometimes visitors are fortunate enough to find wooden carvings of figures, animals and spirit deities. Each region has its own style and these carvings are fascinatingly different from typical African carvings.

Weaving has become a major source of income in many areas, and handworked mohair and woollen tapestries make wonderful gifts. The finest weaving centre is Thorkild Hand Weaving in the industrial suburb of Maseru. Visitors are welcome to watch the weavers work, as they design, dye and then hand-weave beautiful carpets, wall hangings and rugs. Similar goods can also be found at a number of other centres around the country, such as Helang Basali Crafts of Lesotho, at the St Agnes Mission in Teyateyaneng and the Leribe Craft Centre at the junction of the road from Leribe to Butha Buthe.

Common to most southern Africans, Basothos do a great deal of grasswork. The traditional conical Basotho hat is always popular and tiny ones can be bargained for from the hawkers outside the Tourist Office in Maseru. Baskets, place mats, sleeping mats and flower holders can be found in most areas of Lesotho – notice how the grasswork differs from region to region. One of the best ways of protecting grasswork while travelling is to fill the basket or hat with socks or newspaper, place it open end down and then pack clothing around it.

For leather and sheepskin products, the hills and valleys of central and northern Lesotho are the places to go. Although many of the items are transported to Maseru, the mountain towns still have a selection of these goods for sale. The Wool Centre in Mokhotlong appears to have only a few sparsely stocked shelves, but ask the assistant for her "Zimvu" products; you will be shown soft wool-lined slippers and various leather handbags and belts. People unable to reach these distant places should visit the Basotho Tanning Factory in the industrial area of Maseru, telephone (09266) 322618.

Traditionally the Basotho used clay, copper and beads for their jewellery, but this has virtually disappeared in the more modernised areas of the western and southern regions of Lesotho. Imported metals are now worked instead, and are a far cry from the tribal ornaments of the distant villages. The isolated villages between Semonkong and Nkau, and further across along the A4 in the east, are good places to find traditional jewellery work in the form of necklaces and bangles. It often happens in these villages that when asked the price the maker suggests that you name a price. Remember that this is only the start of the haggling, but don't be ridiculous; after all, the products do take considerable time and talent to make.

THINGS TO SELL

Lesotho is short of many Western products, but keep in mind that most of the population live on or below the breadline: you cannot expect to sell luxury items. It will be easy to find a market for your 1 litre of spirits allowed into the country, but beware of encroaching on the territory of the local drinking house. Cigarettes are not a good choice for trying to sell in Lesotho: the quality and price of the tobacco arriving from South Africa are difficult to beat. Warm clothing is quickly bought, especially in the higher districts like Thaba Tseka, Mokhotlong and the larger villages near the Sehlabathebe National Park. Some people are even willing to trade warm clothing for traditional handicrafts – this is a useful way for a visitor to contribute something of value to the Basotho people; while your curio rests on the mantlepiece, the jersey you swopped is worn daily as a protection against the harsh weather of Lesotho.

LANGUAGE

There is no letter "D" in the Sesotho language, and instead the letter "L," although written, is pronounced "D". Many Basothos in the urban centres are able to speak some English, but once in the rural districts visitors will soon need some knowledge of the often tongue-tying Sesotho language. A few of the basic phrases are listed here, but they should only serve as a base from which to learn a greater vocabulary. Most children learn English at school, and they are possibly the best ones to learn more Sesotho from. Initially your efforts may end in disaster as the children roll around on the ground laughing. There is nothing malicious in their mirth; you should just join in the laughter and, with their help, try again.

Greetings – Lumela (pronounced dumela)
Goodbye – Tsamaya hantle
Father – Intate
Mother – Me'
How are you? – Lekae? (pronounced with the "L")
I am well – Ke phetse hantle
Pleased to meet you – Ke thaba ho o bona
Good evening – Robala hantle
What is your name? – Lebitso lahao ke mang?
My name is . . . – Lebitso laka ke . . .
Do you speak English? – Na o bua English?
No – Tjhe'
Yes – Ee
Where is the . . .? – E kae . . .?
What is . . .? – Ke 'ng . . .?
How much is this? – Ke bo kae?
It costs too much – Tefelo ya yona e kgolo
When does the bus leave? – Bus e' tla tsamaya neng?
What is the fare to . . .? – Na leeto le lefellwa bokae . . .?
Does this bus go to . . .? – 'Na bus e', eya kae . . .?
Stop here please – Ema mona ka kopo

3 GETTING THERE

For visitors from Europe there are three ways of reaching Lesotho. All necessitate going through South Africa. Flying is obviously the easiest, quickest and most comfortable method, but the airfare is often high and you miss out on many other countries and experiences. By ship can be a lot of fun and includes stops at interesting ports en route. The problem is that it is often difficult to find work or cabin space available. Third, and the most exciting, is getting to Lesotho overland.

From North and South America, visitors will either have to fly or find passage on a ship. The same is true for visitors arriving from any other destination not on the African continent.

AIR

Spend time researching the various airfares available. Rather than just buying a ticket from any travel agency, phone a few agents and the airline information desks. In Europe, pay a visit to the many "economy" or "bucket" travel shops usually found near universities or colleges. These cater mainly for students but are willing to accommodate non-students as well. Tickets from these shops are often up to 30% cheaper than from normal travel agents, but there are a few problems that need to be considered before purchasing. "Bucket" shops do not always have seats available on the date you want to fly, but they do invariably have something close to that date. If you buy a ticket with fixed departure and return dates, any change in the ticket or dates will require you to pay a handling fee, which is about 10% of the fare. Large cities are the ideal place to track down these cheap travel shops: London, Rome and Amsterdam in particular. Sometimes tickets can be bought from other travellers. Visit the local youth hostels and travellers' restaurants found in most cities. The youth hostel near St Paul's in London often has tickets for sale on its noticeboard. Another good place to try is the youth hostel in Düsseldorf: there are frequently return tickets to Africa on sale. Try to get a direct flight to South Africa. Changing planes anywhere outside Kenya or South Africa is often a time-consuming and always an exasperating procedure.

At Jan Smuts Airport in Johannesburg, South Africa, you must transfer to a Lesotho flight. For trips to Africa, consider getting an open ticket valid for at least 12 months. People are quickly enchanted by the continent and you may find yourself staying longer than you intended. Most airlines flying to South Africa take about 10–15 hours, including a stop in either Cairo or Nairobi.

Visitors travelling from North or South America should not even bother about the flights direct from the Americas to South Africa. The airfares for these flights are costly and the time saving is hardly worth mentioning. Instead, fly first to Europe, then change to one of the several airlines with daily flights to South Africa. A good plan is to write to *Trailfinder Magazine* at 42 Earls Court Road, London, W8 6EJ, England. Magazine staff will send you a copy of their latest price listings on cheap flights to Africa, giving you the choice of buying a ticket to Europe, from where you can get a cheap ticket to Africa.

Australians have the choice of flying direct to either South Africa or Zimbabwe. Once again, the price is prohibitive for most budget travellers. A cheaper choice is to fly to Singapore or Bombay. There are a number of airlines flying from Singapore to Johannesburg, at a price considerably lower than direct from Australia. From Bombay passengers will have to change planes in Zambia before going on to South Africa. There is about a five-hour delay in the changeover and passengers going to Johannesburg are not allowed out of the Lusaka airport building.

Once in South Africa, you will be required to take a connecting flight on one of the airlines serving Lesotho:

Lesotho Airways

Address: P.O. Box 861, Maseru, 100, Lesotho
Telephone: (09266) 312453 (Lesotho)
(011) 9701046 (South Africa)

Airlink Airlines

Telephone: (South Africa) (011) 3942430
(031) 422676

Prices are similar, but visitors should make enquiries about flight schedules.

It is also possible to charter a plane from South Africa to any point in Lesotho, obviously at a much higher price. Contact any of the following concerns in South Africa:

Aviacon, tel. (011) 6591707; Executive Aerospace, toll-free tel. 0800 312177; Regional Air, tel. (011) 8868370; Rossair, tel. (011) 6502980; Turbo Air, tel.(011) 6591312.

SEA

Landlocked by South Africa, Lesotho lies almost 170 km from the nearest ocean. So, visitors arriving by sea will still need to travel overland. Apart from the expensive cruise ships that occasionally berth in South African ports, the only other sea passage is on a freight vessel or yacht.

With the scaling down of most merchant fleets, vacancies are difficult to find, and the days of easily working a passage are over. Yet, for some travellers it is still the cheapest way of getting to South Africa. Contact the Port Captain in the large international harbours and ask whether any vessels have filed passage for southern Africa. Then approach the captain of the ship and tell him of your plans plus any abilities you have that might be useful on board. Some nautical knowledge will obviously help.

South Africa is a stop on the world's cruising routes. Each year large numbers of foreign yachts arrive in South Africa's yachting marinas. The best place in the USA to find yachts departing for South Africa is on the Californian coast in July–October. From Europe (especially Greece) yachts leave in May–August and from Australia and New Zealand in July–September. People planning to travel by yacht should read Alison Muir Bennett's book, *The Hitchhiker's Guide to the Oceans*, Adlard Coles, London, 1990.

OVERLAND

Overland is the true traveller's way of getting to Lesotho. For those starting their epic adventure from Europe, there are two common routes that can be followed. The first begins with a ferry crossing to Algiers, then either motoring, bicycling or hitching into the Sahara to Timbuktu in Mali, and on through Burkina-Faso and Benin to Nigeria. From Nigeria the route swings east into Cameroon and the Central African Republic, then on through Zaïre, Uganda, Kenya, Tanzania, Zambia and Zimbabwe: a total distance of over 20 000 km. Finally you will arrive at the South African border at Beit Bridge; it is about another 900 km south to Lesotho.

The second route starts in Egypt (Cairo), runs south as far as Khartoum in the Sudan, changes direction to avoid the civil war in southern

Sudan, and enters the Central African Republic where it merges with the first route. Estimated at about 13 000 km, the second route takes less time. Africa overlanders should read David Bryon's book, *Africa Overland, a Route and Planning Guide*, Roger Lascelles, Middlesex, 1991.

TO OR FROM SOUTH AFRICA

Hitchhikers will find South Africa ideal for lifts. Visitors with their own transport will discover the best roads in Africa, with numerous filling stations offering good quality fuel – unusual in Africa. To reach Lesotho from Johannesburg, travel east on the N3 freeway to the village of Villiers, then follow the R51 main road to the town of Bethlehem. From Bethlehem take the scenic R26 route south to Ficksburg, 388 km away, and proceed another 47 km to Ladybrand and then into Lesotho.

From the port city of Durban on the east coast of South Africa, take the N3 to Pietermaritzburg, then turn west onto the R617 to Underberg, another 6 km north to Himeville and then up the difficult but spectacular Sani Pass into Lesotho. Total distance is about 170 km. This route is however only recommended for 4x4s, motorbikes and bicycles. During winter it may be closed after heavy snowfalls. Hitching this route is easy; there is a lot of traffic to Himeville, but then you will have to wait for a truck or off-road vehicle going up the Sani Pass. The best time to hitch is early morning. Stand at the T-junction north of Himeville, on the road going to Nottingham Road and the Sani Pass.

From Cape Town on the south-western coast of South Africa it is a long, dry and dusty 1 160 km to the Lesotho border on the Caledon river between Ladybrand and Maseru. Leave Cape Town on the N1 freeway, travelling through the arid Karoo to the city of Bloemfontein. From Bloemfontein it is about 157 km east to Lesotho. This road, sign-posted R64, passes through a part of the so-called homeland of Bophuthatswana (a self-governing state under the auspices of the South African government), then crosses the Maseru Bridge into Lesotho.

4 GETTING AROUND

Lesotho is a difficult country in which to travel. The weather frequently damages roads and airstrips, but with resourcefulness and perseverance it is possible to see most areas of the country. There are several options available and each has its positive and negative aspects. The best method is undoubtedly to travel with your own motorised transport, in the form of a 4x4 vehicle or motorcycle. A few visitors occasionally fly from town to town, while budget travellers prefer public transport, and a few masochists do it by bicycle.

TRAIN

Visitors used to touring by train will be disappointed. Lesotho has one railway station – in the capital, Maseru – and a mere 26 km of railway line in the entire country. The mountains and deep valleys make it impractical to extend the line further. But the real problem is that passenger trains, which formed part of the South African railway system, no longer serve Lesotho.

BUS

To compensate for the lack of rail transport the bus network is well developed, cheap and typically African. Buses serve most areas of Lesotho and provide the main transport for the inhabitants, the slower Basotho ponies having been phased out in the villages near main roads. Though not the safest method of getting around, buses offer a unique opportunity for meeting the locals. Do not expect luxury buses with airconditioning and padded seats. It is safe to say that travelling in Lesotho by bus will be crowded, dirty, noisy and lively. Visitors will be stared at, sniggered at and finally spoken to: it is uncommon for foreign visitors to travel by bus in Lesotho.

No matter how hard you try to blend in, a foreigner stands out. In larger towns with big bus depots, touts will soon be asking your destination and offering all sorts of concessions. Stay calm and choose one of the young men shouting your intended destination. No matter what they said when trying to get you to their bus, fares in Lesotho are under government control. Some travellers have however been asked a higher fare to cover luggage. Check that the destination indicated on the scroll-board is actually where the bus is going; do this by asking the driver, his assistant and a few of the passengers.

The western side of the country between Mafeteng, Maseru and Butha Buthe is well served with buses travelling in both directions. In the central, northern, eastern and south-eastern regions there is usually only one or two buses in either direction each day. Travellers starting their journey from Maseru should ask the Tourist Information Office about departure times. (It's pointless asking arrival times at destinations because any combination of factors could delay the bus.) Another, sometimes notorious, advantage is that buses travel at high speed. During the dry season this means that visitors can quickly cover large distances while still seeing the magnificent scenery and being among the Basotho.

If you are taking one of the night buses that cover the longer routes, such as between Butha Buthe and Mokhotlong, or Maseru and Qacha's Nek, take along some food and drink (traditional food can sometimes be bought at the villages at which the bus stops), warm clothing (crossing the mountain passes is always cold), and a sense of humour. Luggage is packed onto the roofs of buses, together with fruit, animals, beer and blankets. Visitors taking a bus during the rainy season should cover their luggage with black dustbin liners, and remember to pack all belongings inside plastic within the bags. Although the bus-assistant usually ties your luggage to the roof, a good precaution is to check his knots and see what else he may have strapped onto or around your luggage. Theft is unlikely, but at crowded stops check that your bags have not been accidentally thrown off or are being tampered with.

For the adventurer, travelling in Lesotho by bus will provide a rare insight into the lives of the people, their habits, manners and culture. Initially it may require courage, but within a few hours of starting your journey you will realise that it is the best way of getting truly immersed in the experience of Lesotho.

MINIBUS TAXI

If there are heirs to the charioteers of ancient Rome, then they are undoubtedly the minibus taxi drivers of Lesotho. Nicknamed "Zolas" after the South African middle-distance champion Zola Budd, these minibus taxis provide a fast and dangerous alternative to buses.

Minibus taxis have no fare-meters and visitors must negotiate the price before getting into the vehicle. Ask whether the fare covers all your luggage and whether the minibus taxi goes directly to your destination. Minibus taxis do not follow any time schedule, leave when there are at least 19 passengers aboard and have limited luggage space – which means that you will inevitably end up with your bags on your or someone else's lap.

There is a system involved when you want to stop a minibus taxi: stand side-on to the road, with your back towards the direction you want to go. If you are alone and want to go further than 10 km raise your right index finger only. Should you wish to go nearer than 10 km, point your right index finger at the ground. When there is more than one prospective passenger, use two or three fingers (one for each person) pointing as described. Minibus taxis not going the distance you have indicated will not stop, while drivers who are not certain where you want to go will stop and ask.

Once aboard, ignore the maximum passenger sign indicating 12–15 passengers, and try to get comfortable. Talking to fellow travellers is always interesting and makes for hilarious moments as you try not to go squint talking to the person next to you, while squeezed in so tight that you are almost touching noses. As have buses, minibus taxis have stereo systems played at ear-splitting volume. It is no use asking for it to be turned down, the driver and other passengers will loudly dismiss the suggestion anyway.

Minibus taxis are gaining popularity in Lesotho, and for budget travellers they are a good way of covering a number of short "hops" at a cheaper price than one long-distance bus ticket. Foreigners can expect to be given a front seat in the minibus taxi, which, although it may be regarded as a privilege, is not the ideal place to be. Being able to see the road, the traffic and the road-skills of the driver is not something many travellers enjoy, and you may soon find yourself refusing the offer.

AIR

For visitors with limited time, it is sometimes quicker to fly around the country. Notice the word "sometimes": with the unpredictable weather in the interior of Lesotho, flights are frequently delayed. To make matters worse, the bad weather often sets in for days. But the sheer delight or terror that people experience when flying in Lesotho makes most trips in those little planes unforgettable. There are many villages in the country that have no road access, airplanes being their only means of contact with the outside. Do not expect a direct flight to your destination; the plane usually makes a number of stops at remote villages and missions where the landing-strip is little more than a level terrace cut from the hillside. The advantage, though, is that while the pilot is supervising the unloading of post, food, pots and pans, you can wander around settlements that travellers with their own transport seldom reach.

There is a complex grid of flights around Lesotho; most towns have airports and are served almost daily by one or more flights in either direction. Smaller villages are visited less frequently. Lesotho Airways flies propeller-driven aircraft that take between four and eight people with light luggage. A maximum luggage allowance of 20 kg per passenger is strictly enforced. With the difficult and treacherous airstrips, pilots take every precaution necessary.

The best way of getting a flight is to go to the local airstrip and wait. There is an official schedule of times and dates, but this is really more of a rough guide than a definite programme. The routes frequently flown are Maseru–Mokhotlong and Maseru–Qacha's Nek, with a number of stops in between, including places such as Thaba Tseka, Hlotse, Mohale's Hoek and Moyeni (Quthing) – with the most remote stops being at Lesobeng and Lebakeng. Getting friendly with the ground-crew can often be an advantage, and occasionally they manage to get visitors on a private or transport plane. It is possible to book flights from outside the country, but few travellers worry about this.

Unlike internal flights in most other countries, Lesotho Airways domestic flights are surprisingly cheap. They may lack air-hostesses and champagne lunches, but the scenery and flimsiness of the plane will command most of your attention anyway. Patience is required when either booking or waiting for a plane. Often the airstrip will be deserted and the information desk unmanned; nobody seems even to know what a plane is, let alone tell you what's happening. If you plan to fly from airfield to airfield, it is a good idea to take along a "walkman" music system or a good book to read, especially when flying out of Maseru. It is all part of the relaxed Basotho view of life, and if you can accept rather than fight their attitude, you will soon find yourself as unconcerned about delays as they are.

OWN VEHICLE

This is the most common way visitors travel Lesotho. An ordinary saloon car is inadvisable, except in the tarred western areas of the country. Once onto the gravel roads, a car's low ground clearance and lack of power could turn the trip into a series of broken exhausts and getting stuck in the mud. The best vehicle is a strong 4x4. All international driver's licences are accepted, and even a certified translation or copy of your licence is valid in Lesotho for a period of six months.

Avoid overloading by keeping passengers to a maximum of four. It is important to know the vehicle's load capacity and not exceed this. Once off the tar and onto the gravel, driving gets more difficult and an overladen vehicle quickly becomes unstable, especially in the frequent Lesotho thundershowers. Pack the luggage carefully with evenly distributed weight to keep the centre of gravity as low as possible.

Fuel can be a problem on the longer routes, and heavy 4x4s such as Land Rovers and Range Rovers should carry extra fuel in 10 litre cans. This is particularly true for the Drakensberg road from Mokhotlong to Sani Top. Fuel is available in the larger towns and at most tourist resorts, but travellers with motorised vehicles are still advised to fill up their tanks whenever possible. Breakdowns can occur, and when they do it is usually up to the owner to carry out the necessary repairs. A crowd will soon gather – just to watch – the rest is up to you.

Lesotho follows South Africa in driving on the left side of the road. There are speed limits in all areas of the country, but once you are on the gravel, speed limits become irrelevant. Through villages and towns the maximum speed is 60 km/h and on the open road 80 km/h. Avoid the tendency to speed in the wilderness areas: roads are usually wet and slippery. Take particular care when crossing rivers or mountain streams. Their beds are often deceptively deep or soft. Rather attach a rope around someone who then walks across the river ahead of the vehicle.

New spares are expensive and difficult to find. You may have to dig around in a scrapyard for the necessary part. Take along your own essential spares, which should include fan belt, spark plugs, bulbs, two spare tyres, puncture kit, hoses, fuses, electrical wire, accelerator and clutch cable, tyre chains (in winter), a complete and comprehensive tool-kit, tyre levers, tow rope, tyre pressure pump, hydraulic jack, oil and preferably an electric winch.

For trips taken during the cold winter months, make certain that you add anti-freeze to the radiator before you start out. Roads vary from smooth tarred surfaces to the most diabolical potholed obstacle courses. There is no doubt that your driving ability will be tested, and by the end of the journey you will have no need of attending any advanced driver's programme.

Driving at night is dangerous because there are no streetlights except in the larger towns, stray animals are difficult to see and road conditions strain both mind and body. Understand that driving your own vehicle around Lesotho requires low speeds in low gears and a lot of caution. Most of the rural roads are narrow gravel gradings, while the village and town thoroughfares are always crowded with lots of traffic. On longer stretches the only traffic you are likely to meet is overcrowded buses or fearless truckers, and drivers are advised to bow to the philosophy of "might is right".

The disadvantage of having your own vehicle is that it insulates you from the people, so make a point of spending time exploring the villages and towns along the way, on foot.

MOTORCYCLE

With its low fuel consumption, ease of handling and sense of freedom, a motorcycle is arguably the most adventurous way of getting around Lesotho. Visitors choosing this method of travel should not attempt the journey with anything smaller than a 250 cc motorcycle, and preferably a "scrambler" model.

Travelling through Lesotho by motorcycle requires planning, as repair shops are almost nonexistent and spares need to be carried. For travellers on their first major off-road motorcycle trip, it is worthwhile attending a basic maintenance course run by dealers or technical colleges. Get hold of a copy of Ted Simon's informative and fascinating book, *Jupiter's Travels* (Penguin Books, Middlesex, 1988): it covers a four-year journey around the world on a motorcycle and includes hints and tips which could prove valuable in Lesotho.

There is little chance of getting stuck in the mud or sand on a motorcycle, and you are always guaranteed an excited reception. Scattered throughout Lesotho are numerous tracks, paths and trails that, although inaccessible to 4x4s, are within the capabilities of most motorcycles. Lack of security is obviously a disadvantage. Try not to leave the motorcycle other than at a police station, military barracks or with the local village headman.

With the fuel economy of modern motorcycles, riders need not worry about running out of petrol, for example, a Honda XL500S with a full tank of petrol can comfortably cover the 143 km distance between Butha Buthe and Mokhotlong. Some motorcyclists have converted to long-range fuel tanks, but the cost involved is unnecessary for a journey through Lesotho. For safety, however, it is advisable to carry at least 1 litre of petrol in an aluminium canister.

The conventional method of carrying equipment in panniers can present difficulties on the wet and potholed roads of Lesotho. To keep the motorcycle's balance even, travel with a backpack laid flat on the rear section of the seat, and then put your spares bag and tent on top of the pack. Tie-downs are useful, provided they are attached correctly and further strengthened with "octopus" elastics. Spares should include a comprehensive tool-kit, at least two inner tyre tubes, blow-weld temporary puncture repair, puncture repair kit, tyre levers, clutch, brake and throttle cables, spark plug, globes, main fuse, a 500 ml can of oil, chain master-links, foot pump and length of rope.

Safety should be an important consideration for motorcyclists. Basotho drivers all seem bent on dashing about at the greatest possible speed, irrespective of who is on the road. Fit your two rearview mirrors with small blind-spot mirrors, check that lights are working and that there are sufficient reflectors on the front, sides and back of the motorcycle. Avoid riding after sunset, especially in the remote regions where a breakdown or accident could leave you stranded for a long time before help arrives.

Visitors using motorcycles will experience the whole diversity of Basotho life, numerous adventures, misadventures, breakdowns, arguments, cold, discomfort, excitement and joy. A motorcycle offers a wonderful opportunity for touring the isolated areas of Lesotho and provides an experience that, once taken, will be magical.

BICYCLE

Bicycles are a rarity in Lesotho – mainly because of the many mountains, hills, unbridged rivers and steep valleys that make up most of the country. Travelling in Lesotho by bicycle requires physical fitness and mental strength. You will be faced with high mountain passes, grass tracks, tarred roads and gravel paths that wind past villages and through hill towns. Cycling does however have the dubious advantage of, apart from walking the whole way, being the cheapest method of getting around the country.

In the western districts of Lesotho it is easy to find a place to have your bike repaired, but once east of Maseru, Butha Buthe or Mafeteng the responsibility becomes yours. Contact one of the local cycling clubs at home before you start out: they often have useful advice for long-distance cyclists. Neil Clough's book, *Two-Wheel Trek* (Arrow Books, London, 1983), has a number of useful hints for cyclists in Africa.

Expect a crowd wherever you stop, and keep an eye on your luggage. Preferably take an old bicycle to Lesotho: you will no doubt take the odd fall, and the treacherous roads will soon have stones chipping the paint and ruining the mudguards. Become familiar with the mechanics of your bike and its repair before you set out. Take at least the following spares: handpump, puncture repair kit, inner tubes, at least 10 spokes, brake and gear cables, a basic bike tool-kit, chain and derailleur parts. Quick release attachments on your wheels are an advantage when you have to repair punctures, especially outdoors in the rain or snow.

Security, as on a motorcycle, can present problems. The idea of having panniers still remains the best for a bicycle – but remember to take them off whenever you leave the bicycle unattended. A length of chain with a combination lock is useful, but it is more advisable to lock your bike away before you explore on foot.

For people used to racing bicycles: the tyres on these bikes are totally unsuitable for Lesotho's roads, and it will be essential to change the thin, frail tyres and rims for a heavy-duty pair with a criss-cross tread pattern.

Cycling in Lesotho may be frustrating, but it is always exciting; tribesmen who have probably never seen a bicycle will offer you advice on how to repair and ride it, children will want lifts, women will stare in amazement, and mountain winds will by turns push you along and wear you down. Cyclists have occasionally reported incidents of stone throwing by schoolchildren. Try to see this for what it is – a stranger comes hurtling through the schoolyard on a seldom seen contraption: is it real, dangerous or an apparition? – and instead of stopping in anger, just ride on.

If most of your cycling experience has been on mountain bicycles, Lesotho will provide an interesting challenge. Get fit before attempting the journey; the usual two to three-hour ride on the weekend will not adequately prepare you for the difficulties of cycling in the mountains of Lesotho. Work out a pre-trip programme and try to cover at least 30–50 km per day, with lots of hill work on sand or dirt roads. The best part of touring Lesotho by bicycle is not having to worry about departure times or fuel, which allows you to stop wherever and whenever you like.

For more information on mountainbiking in Lesotho, contact Alistair at (09266) 323166, Maseru. Buy a topographical map from the Department of Surveys, P.O. Box 876, Maseru, 100, Lesotho.

HITCHHIKING

Hitchhiking around Lesotho is easy and fun, although in the northern and eastern parts of the country lifts can be hard to come by. There are many vehicles travelling in the other regions and visitors can expect quick lifts. Do not expect to be given a lift in any of the aid organisation vehicles: these seem reserved exclusively for their own workers, and travellers are regarded as little more than users and exploiters of the country. Instead, you will find yourself getting most of your lifts on the back of trucks and in overloaded vans.

Foreigners seldom hitchhike around Lesotho, and the locals are always amused and interested in those who do. Sitting in the open on the back of a truck has distinct advantages: it offers an unobstructed view of the countryside, there are inevitably other passengers to meet and the ride is usually free. It is nevertheless good policy to ask the driver whether he expects payment. Forget about the accepted way of hitching by sticking out your thumb – the result is only laughter – rather keep your hand horizontal and wave it up and down to stop an approaching vehicle.

Try to be at a main road or truck-stop early in the morning, when most long-distance transport leaves. Standing at the entrance or exit of towns has also proved a useful way of getting lifts. Alternatively tour the local eating and drinking houses the night before, and ask among the revellers whether any trucks or vehicles are travelling your route the next day. On less populated routes try for a through ride, or you may find yourself facing a long walk or sleeping out. (Neither is pleasant in the harsh weather of Lesotho.)

No matter what distance you intend covering, you will usually be asked to visit a village en route and sometimes to spend the night. Take advantage of this offer: it is a good chance to mix with the locals, share their food and homes and expand your mind to encompass other views. Be careful of accepting lifts in and out of Lesotho: there is drug trafficking across the borders with South Africa, and you could land up in a serious situation. Instead, walk across the border and then hitch a lift once in Lesotho. With the alcohol abuse in Lesotho, be wary of accepting lifts in vehicles where the driver or the passengers are obviously drunk.

Hitching rides around the eastern side of Lesotho is difficult, as there is little traffic – most of the area is served by airplane. Especially difficult is the section from Mokhotlong to Qacha's Nek, and visitors should rather hitch first to Thaba Tseka and then south to Qacha's Nek.

An alternative to hitchhiking is a combination of hitching and pony-riding. This does take longer but is a lot more fun than just hitchhiking. Hitching in Lesotho requires a mercenary attitude and an ability to handle discomfort, but it also exposes you to the trauma that many Basotho experience as they are being torn between the traditional and modern. It is not uncommon to get a ride in a new 4x4 that is filled with four or five blanketed shepherds, one or two of their sheep and a bale of hay.

ORGANISED TOURS

In comparison to the highly developed tourism industry in neighbouring South Africa, Lesotho has few organised tours or tour operators. The Lesotho Tourist Board in Maseru is able to arrange local tours of the capital and immediate surroundings. Within Lesotho, some of the hotels and lodges can arrange guides, ponies and transport. Visitors hoping to travel further with a tour company need to make arrangements in South Africa. The choice is limited, but possibilities are:

Drifters (pony-trekking tours)

Address: P.O. Box 48434, Roosevelt Park, 2129, South Africa
Telephone: (011) 8881160 or 7839200

Overland Safaris (round-country trips and pony-trails)

Address: P.O. Box 82, Warden, 9890, South Africa
Telephone: (014372) ask for 646 or 3521

Organised tours have the advantage of everything being planned and laid out for you. The disadvantage, though, is that you seldom get to meet your fellow tourists prior to the trip, which could lead to clashes later on. Also, by being in a common group you may miss out on the contact with locals; you are constantly being reminded of the difference between the Basotho and yourself: a wall exists, with you being only an observer.

Few tours are being run by the companies that do arrange visits to Lesotho, and visitors should consider a less expensive but more adventurous way of seeing the country.

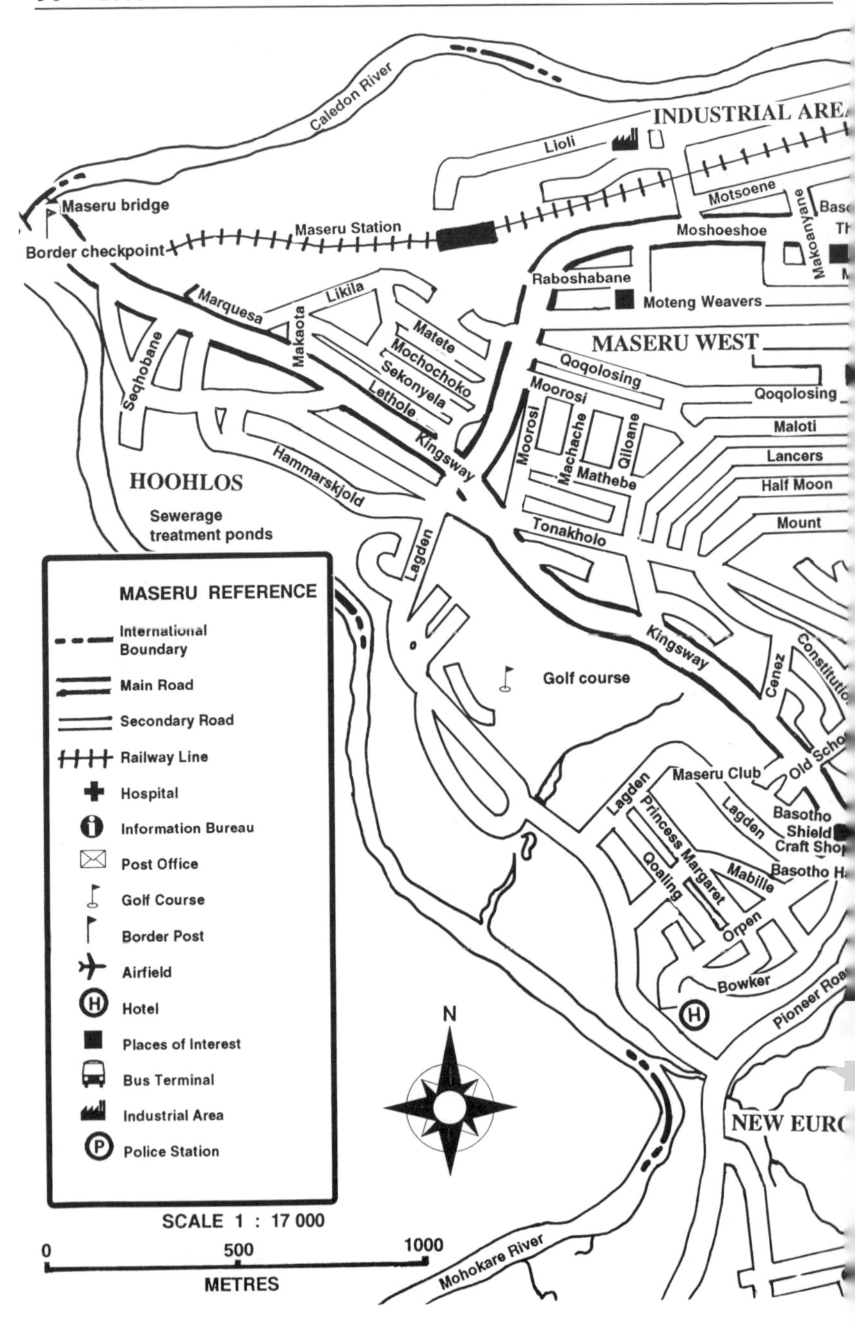
Caledon River
INDUSTRIAL AREA
Lioli
Motsoene
Maseru bridge
Border checkpoint
Maseru Station
Moshoeshoe
Makoanyane
Raboshabane
Moteng Weavers
Marquesa
Likila
Makaota
Matete
Mochochoko
Sekonyela
Lethole
Seqhobane
MASERU WEST
Qoqolosing
Moorosi
Machache
Qiloane
Mathebe
Maloti
Lancers
Half Moon
Mount
Kingsway
HOOHLOS
Hammarskjold
Sewerage treatment ponds
Tonakholo
Lagden
Golf course
Cenez
Maseru Club
Princess Margaret
Qoaling
Mabille
Basotho Shield Craft Shop
Orpen
Bowker
Pioneer Road
NEW EURO
Mohokare River
N
MASERU REFERENCE
International Boundary
Main Road
Secondary Road
Railway Line
Hospital
Information Bureau
Post Office
Golf Course
Border Post
Airfield
Hotel
Places of Interest
Bus Terminal
Industrial Area
Police Station
SCALE 1 : 17 000
0
500
1000
METRES

Reservoir
SOUTH AFRICA
LESOTHO
Jewellery
MOSHOESHOE
Thatho
Joele
Molapo
Seeiso
Accacia
Majara
Maama
Coronation Square
Leloko
Letlatsa
Mopeli
Sekhonyana
Oxbow
Mamathe
Baring
Mohokare River
Matlama
SEA POINT
Moshoeshoe road
Phamola
Molomoamphi
Short
Cemetery
Mantsebo
Berea
Evelyn
Airport
Seputana
Mejametalana Airport
Papashane
Piet Sello
STADIUM
Fako
Motsamai
Sekese
Mafole
Phamola
Rantsala
Setsoto Stadium
& St James
n Cathedral
Reservoir
Assissi
Moshoeshoe Road
al Palace
Depart of Tourism
Maseela
Airport
Ramafole
Lechesa
Ntsane
Lerotholi
Linare
Parliament
Palace
Masia
Stadium
Tlebere
Pitso Ground
Parkside Cinema
Constitution
Airport
Central Park
Pitso
Bus Terminal
Market
Queen Elizabeth II Hospital
Kingsway
Main North 1
Teyateyaneng
hoe's
Sanlam Centre
Sports Ground
High Court
Roman Catholic Cathedral of Our Lady of Victories
CATHEDRAL
Lesotho Sun
EUROPA 1
Nightingale
Mabekebeke
Main South 1
Kuene
Thebe
Bus terminal
Nightingale
SVIEW
To Roma & Mafeteng

5 MASERU

Maseru is a sprawling mass of humanity, buildings and traffic. Visitors arriving in the capital after exploring other regions are often dazed by the change. There is a clash of cultures, beliefs and ideas that results in a vibrant mixture of African, European and Asian influences visible throughout the city. You will see men on ponies vying for a lane with the latest German motorcar. From tinted-glass office blocks in the city centre to stone and thatch huts 100 m beyond the sumptuous Lakeside Hotel, Maseru will captivate and fascinate visitors.

Maseru (the name of the red sandstone found in the area) was the seat of the British, who arrived in 1869 to exploit their Protectorate rights. Today visitors can still see some of the original British buildings. Maseru lies on the Caledon river border with South Africa, and is the paramount trading centre for the whole country. But with an economic recession biting hard into one of the poorest countries on earth, the population of Maseru is swelling daily. Shanty towns are springing up everywhere, especially around the market area. Because of the tide of traffic and people many of the roads are potholed and damaged. Alleys are smeared with effluent and, unheard of until recently, beggars pester passersby. The City Council is trying desperately to rectify the problems, and construction is seen almost everywhere.

ORIENTATION

Built in an east-west direction, Maseru lies in a shallow valley on a meandering bend of the Caledon river. Entering from north or south, travellers will find Cathedral Circle the gateway to the city. From the Maseru Bridge border post with South Africa, the road runs into the business thoroughfare of Kingsway. Finding your way around Maseru is confusing and often frustrating. Trying to do it from your own vehicle, while fighting the traffic congestion, is virtually impossible.

Of importance to travellers is the area along Kingsway, about 2 km to the west of Our Lady of Victories Cathedral. This is the modern part of Maseru and is also the location of banks, handicraft shops, the main post office, hotels and restaurants. The first road to the right, east of the post office, leads to a park where the founder of Lesotho, Moshoeshoe, is honoured by a statue.

From Cathedral Circle, the road south is Main South 1. This road passes through the newer but poorer suburbs of Maseru. To the northwest of Cathedral Circle is Moshoeshoe Road, which runs parallel to Kingsway and leads to the industrial area and the only railway station in Lesotho. If arriving on a Friday afternoon or Saturday morning, visitors with their own transport can avoid the chaos of Kingsway by taking this road until it curves to join Kingsway at the western end of the business district. Main North 1 heads out of the city towards Teyateyaneng and the mountain moorlands of northern Lesotho.

Getting around Maseru is best done on foot, though any of the numerous minibus taxis that dash about the city can be flagged down and a lift taken to your destination. Parking can be a problem for those with their own transport and most visitors leave their vehicles at an hotel or the RLMP (police) on Constitution Road.

INFORMATION

Information can be obtained from the Lesotho Tourist Office (tel. 322892 or 323760) on Kingsway, beneath the Hotel Victoria. Office hours are Monday to Friday 08h00–17h00 and Saturday 08h00–13h00. The staff are fluent in a number of languages, helpful and well-informed. Ask for the free Lesotho Map, which includes a detailed plan of Maseru. Pamphlets are also available which advertise hotels, lodges, curios and tours. Another useful piece of literature, if you intend spending a few days in the capital, is the latest issue of *What's On In Maseru*. For more detailed information visit the Ministry of Tourism on Linare Road; to find these offices, follow Kingsway as far as the traffic lights at the entrance to the Queen Elizabeth II Hospital. Turn into Parliament Road for one block and then left into Constitution Road; Linare is the first road to the right. The Tourism Office is on the top floor of the modern brown building about 50 m from the corner. Staff here are able to provide visitors with a great deal more information than the Tourist Office on Kingway. As the Ministry is hopelessly understaffed, visitors should make a prior appointment, at least two weeks in advance. Telephone: (09266) 323734, Monday to Friday 08h00–12h45 and 14h00–16h30. Or write to: Ministry of Tourism, Sports and Culture, P.O. Box 52, Maseru, 100, Lesotho.

The main post office is east of Lancer's Inn on Kingsway. Open from 08h00–16h30, this is the best post office for making international calls and receiving poste restante mail. If you are expecting a letter or parcel, go to the parcel counter to the left of the main door. Request the poste restante box and be prepared for a search. If you cannot find your letter ask to see the foreign-parcel shelves – a number of travellers have reported finding their letters under parcels marked with the same first letter as their surname! International calls can be arranged by speaking to either the Postmaster or his assistant.

Some major international banks have branches in Maseru, and changing traveller's cheques and hard currency or drawing cash with a credit card can be done quickly and efficiently. A reliable way of having money sent to you is by telexing the amount to the bank. Using this method saves hours of paperwork and identification at the post office. The banks are:

Standard Chartered Bank (Africa PLC)

Physical address: Kingsway Central
Postal address: Maseru Branch, P.O. Box 4, Maseru, 100, Lesotho
Telephone: 322575, fax 310025, telex 4332 SCBMA LO

Barclays Bank PLC

Physical address: 1st Floor, Bank Building, Kingsway Town Centre, Kingsway
Postal address: P.O. Box 115, Maseru, 100, Lesotho
Telephone: 312423, fax 310068, telex 4346 LO, telegrams Barcladom

Lesotho Bank

Physical address: Lesotho Bank Tower Block, Kingsway
Postal address: Central Services Maseru, P.O. Box 1053, Maseru, 100, Lesotho
Telephone: 315737, fax 310268, telex 4206 LO

American Express Travel

Physical address: Central Kingsway
Postal address: P.O. Box 294, Maseru, 100, Lesotho
Telephone: 312554, fax 310216, telex 4334 AMEX LO

On the same side of Kingsway as the post office, this is a good place for having mail sent, cashing traveller's cheques and meeting other travellers.

For visitors flying around Lesotho, Maseru is the only place where you can pre-book tickets. Remember that this does not guarantee that you will fly on that particular date at that time – it all depends on the notorious mountain weather. Unlike many other African countries, Lesotho does not have different prices for foreigners and locals; everybody pays the same price. Payment can be made in any internationally accepted currency, by traveller's cheque or credit card. Personal cheques are seldom accepted and even company cheques may be refused. Airline offices:

Lesotho Airways

Physical address: Reservations and Sales, Central Business District, Maseru
Postal address: P.O. Box 861, Maseru, 100, Lesotho
Telephone: 314507 or 312453, fax 310126, telex 4389 LO

Air Maluti

Physical address: Make bookings either at the Airport Building at Moshoeshoe International Airport or at the Maseru Sun Cabanas Complex on Orpen Road
Postal address: Private Bag A386, Maseru, 100, Lesotho
Telephone: 312813 or 3350314, fax 310130

The latest movies can be seen at the dilapidated Kingsway Cinema near the Tourist Office and Hotel Victoria, and the Parkside Cinema on the corner of Airport and Parliament roads. Get there early, especially on Friday evenings or for Saturday shows.

The American Cultural Centre (tel. 312335) is in the LNDC Shopping Centre on Kingsway. There is a library containing numerous American books and magazines, and a helpful information service.

The British Council (tel. 312609) is near the corner of Kingsway and Lerotholi Road, and is a good place to catch up on the latest British and European news. The library has a large selection of books, videos and magazines.

Photographic film can be bought and developed in Maseru from CNA on Kingsway, about 20 m east of the Tourist Information Centre, and Hollywood Photo in the Bedco Centre Building near Maseru's central business district. While the CNA photo-developing takes a day or two, Hollywood Photo claims to develop your photos the same day. Get your exposed films in for developing as early as possible in the morning.

Basic camera repairs are undertaken at Candifotos, 1st Floor, Fairways Centre, Kingsway (tel. 325034).

Books, magazines and the latest South African newspapers can be bought from CNA on Kingsway. Avoid trying to buy something from this shop at lunchtime or on Saturday mornings; the shop is then full of casual readers and queues of shoppers. There is also a research library on Kingsway, near the Standard Chartered Bank. The literature on Lesotho is limited but the librarians can find you information on most aspects of Lesotho.

Emergency contacts in Maseru are:

Royal Lesotho Mounted Police (RLMP)
On Constitution Road, between Lerotholi and Palace roads about 30 m north of the British Council
Telephone: 124 or 123

Maseru Fire Brigade
Telephone: 122 (all areas throughout Lesotho have the same fire brigade number)
Chief Fire Officer (tel. 326350)

Maseru Ambulance Service
Telephone: 121 (This service is far from reliable and unless it is a matter of life and death visitors are better advised to get themselves to a hospital.)
Maseru has six hospitals. Foreigners are allowed to attend these; payment must be made and then claimed from medical insurance. Serious diseases and surgery are referred to a South African hospital. If the illness or injury is life-threatening, patients are transported by the Lesotho Flying Doctor Service. The best equipped hospital, with the largest number of trained staff, is the Queen Elizabeth II Hospital on Kingsway (tel. 121 or 322501).

Several pharmacies serve the Maseru community, most of which have well-stocked prescription drug facilities. Prescriptions are seldom checked, and even scheduled drugs can be bought over the counter.

Allied Chemists
Ground Floor, Allied Building, Pitso
Telephone: 322786
Also at the LNDC Centre, Central Maseru
Telephone: 324775

Cathedral Pharmacy

Tlelai Building, Main North 1 Road, near Cathedral Circle, Maseru
Telephone: 324351

Lesmed Pharmacy

New Agricultural Bank Building, Kingsway, Maseru
Telephone: 317804

Doctors and dentists can be found by contacting one of the embassies in Maseru. Both British and American embassies have lists of recommended doctors used by their staff and suitable for foreign visitors. Traditional healers are gaining popularity, and there is a growing tendency for "Western" doctors to liaise with traditional healers. Interestingly, it has been proven that some Basotho traditional healers can cure certain types of cancer. Herb preparations are available from the market at Central Park near Cathedral Circle, and also around Pitso Ground on Market Road. Contact the Ministry of Health (tel. 324404) for information on where to find traditional healers, aromatherapists and acupuncture practitioners.

Public transport in and out of Maseru is found mainly in two areas. Buses and minibus taxis departing for the southern and central regions of Lesotho go out along the Main South 1 from about 1 km past Our Lady of Victories Cathedral. The terminal is an open gravel area on the right, next to a school. For public transport to the north, walk north from Cathedral Circle along Main North 1 for about 200 m and then turn left into Pitso Road. Where Pitso is intersected by Market Road, turn right. The bus and minibus taxi depot is there in the chaos of street vendors, wooden stalls and crowds of travellers. At both places it will be necessary to ask drivers where you can find the transport going your way. This can take time, especially over weekends – buy yourself a roasted corn on the cob and begin the search. If leaving Maseru, get to the depot early. This is when most long-distance buses and minibus taxis depart.

Fuel is available from a number of filling stations throughout the city. Drivers need just drive in any direction from Cathedral Circle to be certain of finding a fuel supply. Check that the bowser has been reset before your tank is filled; there have been reports of foreigners being overcharged.

Hitchhiking into or out of Maseru can be a problem. If you are hitching into the capital, ask your lift to drop you off either at Cathedral Circle or near the post office in the centre of the central business district.

Getting out of Maseru by hitching is difficult, and it is better to take a minibus taxi out of the city for about 5 km along either Main North 1 or Main South 1, depending on the direction you plan to travel. The Moshoeshoe International Airport is about 20 km south of the city, and there is frequent public transport to and from the airport throughout the day and in the early evening; this depends on the number of flights on that day.

Cars and other vehicles can be rented from any of the rent-a-car outlets, but unless you are planning to use the vehicle to travel outside the capital, this is not recommended, because of the large number of hit-and-run accidents that occur in the crowded and congested streets of Maseru.

Avis Rent-a-Car

Kingsway, central Maseru
Telephone: 314325 or 312554, fax 310216
Also at Moshoeshoe International Airport
Telephone: 350326, fax 350011

Hertz Executive Car Hire

Ground Floor, Lesotho Sun Hotel, Hilton Road, Maseru
Telephone: 314460 or 325946, fax 315945, telex 4289 LO

Visa renewals and applications for visitors staying longer than 30 days can be made in the sandstone building on the corner of Kingsway and Palace Road. Although the outside of the building is marked as the Post Office this is actually the Department of Immigration and Passport Services (tel. 322187). Trying to get a visa on Monday or Friday is a total waste of time; rather try Wednesday or Thursday when the staff seem to be at their peak of efficiency. Should you experience difficulties with the service you receive, ask to speak to the Director of Immigration.

Maseru has a few travel agencies that might interest visitors. For touring the country travellers should contact the Tourist Information Centre on Kingsway.

C.S. Travel

Private Bag Z0026, Maseru West
Telephone: 311417

Execu Travel

P.O. Box 1026, Maseru, 100
Telephone: 325113

International Travel and Freight Services
Maseru Book Centre, Kingsway, P.O. Box 294, Maseru, 100
Telephone: 312554, fax 310216, telex 4334 LO

PLACES TO STAY

Maseru is without doubt the most expensive place to stay in Lesotho. Rates cover room only, and meals are expensive. Visitors can expect to pay tariffs that are on a par with top First-World hotels in South Africa. Service is poor and hotels are crowded with prostitutes, openly plying their trade in bars and lounges. There is not a wide price range or selection, and other than in the cheap but awkwardly placed Youth Hostel, visitors are forced to stay at one of the hotels. Camping is not permissible anywhere in the city, and although hotels advertise camping, they seldom allow it unless the hotel is full.

Hotel Victoria (high tariff)

Located across from the Basotho Hat and Craft Shop near the busiest stretch of Kingsway, this hotel is part of the Lesotho Hotels group. Clean and undeniably tourist-orientated, it has 102 rooms, all with bathrooms en suite. There are also four family suites at a rather inflated price. All rooms have television, telephone and airconditioning. There is a swimming pool – usually overcrowded with locals. Three bars serve the hotel, as does a nightclub and beer-garden. The dining room is something of a legend in Maseru, and visitors can enjoy a good selection of food. Curio shops and boutiques litter the hotel, and downstairs is the Kingsway cinema and Tourist Information Office. An advantage of staying at the Hotel Victoria is that transport is laid on for guests to the Pony-trekking Centre near the group's lodge at Molimo-Nthuse.

Postal address: Hotel Victoria, P.O. Box 212, Maseru, 100, Lesotho
Telephone: (09266) 322002, telex 4350 LO

Lancer's Inn (high tariff)

This inn is situated in the centre of Maseru, behind St John's church and the original library. It is a popular stop for travellers and business people alike. Accommodation is in rondavels and bungalows. There are 34 rooms, all with ablution facilities. For guests planning to stay longer than 30 days, self-catering suites can be arranged. Two public bars and a private bar serve the inn, but in reality the private bar is also public and guests share with the locals who crowd the inn. Behind the foyer is a quiet garden which provides sanctuary from the noise and pollution of the inner city. There is no separate dining room and guests are required to take their meals in the cosy Rendezvous Restaurant. Outside is a patio where light meals, tea and coffee are served throughout the day. Studio One Nightclub is an attraction over weekends, and visitors should not miss the opportunity of attending. Guest parking is provided in an enclosed yard with 24-hour security. The staff can be abrupt, few of them speak English and they seem to regard themselves as doing you the favour. The major attraction of Lancer's Inn is its central location and festive atmosphere, particularly on Friday and Saturday evenings.

Postal address: Lancer's Inn, Private Bag A216, Maseru, Lesotho
Telephone: (09266) 312114

Lesotho Sun Hotel (high tariff)

This luxury hotel, off Nightingale Road behind the Queen Elizabeth II Hospital, is aimed at the well-heeled tourist. Built in a large rolling parkland the hotel is visited by foreign consultants and government officials. There are 236 rooms all with private bathrooms. Of these rooms two are lavish royal suites, 216 have double beds and 17 are executive suites. All rooms have television, radio, telephone and air-conditioning. Transport to and from Moshoeshoe International Airport is provided for guests, and non-residents may use the courtesy bus at a small fee. A medical suite is housed at the hotel, as is the Nala Cafe for light meals, while the Lehaha Grill offers full menus. Once the destination of gambling-deprived South Africans, the casino has all the facilities common to other international casinos. To complete the luxury, there are two tennis courts, a gym, sauna, jogging track, swimming pool and, always popular, a ten-pin bowling alley. Reservations should be made well in advance.

Postal address: Reservations Manager, Lesotho Sun Hotel, Private Bag A68, Maseru, Lesotho
Telephone: (09266) 313111

Maseru Sun Cabanas (high tariff)

This hotel lies at the end of Orpen Road, which passes between the Basotho Hat and Craft Shop and the Basotho Shield Craft Shop, and is only a 10 minute walk from the centre of Maseru. Advertised as luxury accommodation, the hotel provides local and country tours for guests, but their availability seems to depend on how long you plan to stay at the cabanas. All 112 rooms have bathrooms, telephones and television. There are bars and gambling amenities, and visitors can enjoy meals in the restaurant. Residents also have the use of a swimming pool, sauna, tennis and volleyball courts. Equipment may be hired or is supplied free for use at the facilities. Hair and beauty salons are also part of the complex and guests who intend using these should make an appointment either at the shop or through the reception desk.

Postal address: Sun International Reservations Manager, Maseru Sun Cabanas, Private Bag A84, Maseru, 100, Lesotho
Telephone: (09266) 312434 or Johannesburg (011) 7838660

Lakeside Hotel (high tariff)

This hotel is 3 km from the centre of Maseru along the Main North 1, set amidst a jumble of houses and light industries. There is plenty of transport to and from the area around the hotel, but most guests appear to have their own transport anyway. When visiting the inner city leave your vehicle at the hotel and use the courtesy bus. Isolated from mainstream Maseru, the Lakeside Hotel is not as popular as other hotels. There are 54 rooms, all with bathroom, television, telephone, radio and airconditioning. For guests who enjoy a drink, the Lakeside Hotel provides a choice of five bars. Expensive but tasty meals are served in the hotel's restaurant and dining room. Because the hotel is used mainly as a conference centre, the staff are untrained in customer service, and visitors need patience when dealing with staff members who often seem rude.

Postal address: The Hotel Manager, P.O. Box 602, Maseru, 100, Lesotho
Telephone: (09266) 313646

Youth Hostel (medium tariff)

About 5 km north of Maseru city, on the road to Lancer's Gap, is the Phomolong Youth Hostel. There is a tiny sign indicating the hostel, but visitors should look for the nursery school on the opposite side of the road about three-quarters of the way to Lancer's Gap. The hostel is frequently full, especially during school terms, and travellers who intend staying there should make reservations a few days in advance. Accommodation is available for 60 guests; no meals are provided. Residents do however have access to the comprehensive kitchen. Water is a problem and you cannot expect a hot wash unless you are very fortunate. Foreign visitors are often invited to join some of the Basotho residents of the hostel on party-trips into Maseru. This is the best way of getting to know the real Maseru.

Volunteer accommodation (low tariff)

Visitors who arrive by hitchhiking or public transport, and have all their belongings in a backpack, are sometimes accommodated at one of the volunteer centres in Maseru. Try contacting the head of the Danish Volunteer Service (tel. 312879) on Mabille Road: this is the second road on the right when travelling up Orpen Road from Kingsway. They can usually organise you a bed for the night. A contribution is always gladly accepted and goes a long way towards making it easier for future travellers to find accommodation. Rooms can also sometimes be found through the Anglican church (tel. 322426 or 324256). For a place to pitch your tent, try the U.S. Peace Corps Office (tel. 313871) near Constitution Road. There are other organisations where travellers can find a bed or room for the night, but remember that these are not hotels and you should move on as soon as possible.

PLACES TO EAT

For those who enjoy eating, Maseru will be a delight. There are numerous restaurants, cafés, take-aways and street stalls. There is something for almost every taste, though vegetarians must accept that the Basotho are predominantly a meat eating population. A wide selection of food is available, from traditional Basotho fare to the latest European cuisine, from bland and dull boiled vegetables to mouth-burning curried chicken. Luxury-trip visitors can enjoy sumptuous five-course meals at any of the hotels, while budget travellers can find filling, tasty and cheap meals in the streets and market areas of Maseru.

Expensive

Auberge Restaurant (tel. 312775) serves tasty, if expensive, meals. The speciality is French cuisine, but there are also dishes of a more international flavour. Popular with business people; lunch-times can be hectic and seating unavailable. Evenings are a lot quieter, and there is a wonderful ambience in the little restaurant. It is a good idea to make prior reservations. To get there, go along Kingsway to the traffic lights at Parliament Road – the restaurant is on the corner across from the Queen Elizabeth II Hospital. Parking is available near the restaurant at the Parkside Cinema.

Boccaccio Restaurant (tel. 325853) is claimed to be Maseru's most popular restaurant; it is also the cheapest of Maseru's top restaurants. With a wide selection of mainly Italian foods, visitors will find generous helpings and excellent service. Run by the Italian owner, the restaurant has a touch of Italy; from the soft Italian music to the traditional little espresso cups. Lunchtime is the busiest period at the Boccaccio and people wanting to eat without a reservation should arrive, at the latest, about 12h30. Tucked behind the Basotho Hat Craft shop on Orpen Road, this restaurant is well situated a few minutes from the centre of town. Parking is available outside the front door of the restaurant.

Dining Room of the Hotel Victoria (tel. 312992). Part of the hotel complex on Kingsway, above the Tourist Information Centre, this restaurant or dining room serves interesting traditional Basotho meals on Wednesday. The staff are well trained and courteous, with a genteel manner seldom seen in other hotel dining rooms. Judging by the number of foreigners who eat here, this must rate as one of the top restaurants in Lesotho. Reservations are not necessary as the large dining room can accommodate well over 50 people at one sitting.

Medium-priced

Lancer's Inn Rendezvous Restaurant and Dining Room (tel. 312114) is a popular restaurant with expatriates and foreign aid-workers; visitors will find few locals eating here. There is a well-prepared carvery at a moderate price, a good à la carte menu and a comprehensive wine list. The service is slow and orders are regularly muddled up, but with patience and an understanding of the local customs, visitors will be able to enjoy the restaurant as much for its food as for its African decor. It is advisable to book for evening meals. The restaurant is to the left of the main Lancer's Inn entrance, behind St John's church on Kingsway.

LeHaha Grill (tel. 313111) is an à la carte restaurant of the Lesotho Sun Hotel on the hill behind the Queen Elizabeth II Hospital. Meals are reasonably priced, and most are also available at lunchtime around the hotel's swimming pool. Frequented by Maseru's more affluent Basothos, this is a good place to see the vast differences that exist in Lesotho. The LeHaha Grill is an ideal place to splash out on a big meal.

Budget travellers seldom have privacy while visiting a country, and the quiet tranquillity of this restaurant is both relaxing and enjoyable. Visitors should book a few hours or, if possible, days ahead, especially during the festive season and over weekends.

Inexpensive

For cheap meals or a snack while on the move, the area to check is around the bus terminal at Pitso Ground, on the corner of Market and Pitso roads. There are literally hundreds of street vendors. They sell a wide choice of food – try the mutton stew with papad. These meals and snacks are all very cheap, and it's almost a crime to expect these people to make a living from what they sell. Fresh fruit and vegetables can also be bought in the market. This is an interesting experience in itself, and takes time as the buyer and seller negotiate over the purchase: the seller will explain why you should buy the products, after which you are expected to make either a happy or sad face – it is the expression on your face that will decide the price you will be charged. (Watch a few of the locals buying fresh produce before you attempt it; it takes practice.) An unusual snack to try while you are walking around the city is roasted corn on the cob, which can be bought from street sellers along Kingsway near the post office.

Fast-food shops have flourished in the city, and hungry visitors will not have to go far without finding at least one. They offer the usual fried food from typically American menus. The pastry shop at the Lancer's Inn makes delicious fresh cakes and pies, and a pie washed down with a litre of milk makes for a filling meal as you sit in the garden of St John's church. There is a lack of traditional Basotho restaurants in Maseru, and visitors will have to travel a few kilometres out of the city to find meals of porridge with chicken or mutton, eaten with the fingers.

To travellers having just arrived from the rural districts, Maseru will seem like a food paradise. And for those still preparing to go into the mountains, this will be your last chance for a long time of such a wide choice of restaurants and foods.

THINGS TO BUY

Maseru has everything the curio hunter could want. Most traditional crafts can be bought in Maseru, and although the prices are much higher than in the rural areas, visitors do not have to travel through wind, rain and sun to find a particular item – they are almost all available in

Maseru. Most of the tourist shops are in the central business district of Maseru, around the Tourist Information Centre on Kingsway. Visitors cannot bargain at the curio shops in Maseru and for travellers just starting their trip, it is advisable to look for the same, but a lot cheaper, items in the rural towns and villages.

Many of the hotels also have curio shops but, unless you have forgotten to buy a memento of Lesotho, their prices are prohibitively high. Get a copy of the "Handicrafts in Lesotho" brochure from the Tourist Information Centre. The whole range of crafted products, from basketware to traditional hats, pottery to tapestries, can be found at the Basotho Shield Craft and Basotho Hat Craft shops on the corner of Orpen road and Kingsway (tel. 322458).

Excellent mohair and woollen woven products can be bought in Maseru. These are all handmade by people who work under a carefully controlled co-operative scheme. Many of the workshops are open to the public and visitors can spend a few interesting hours watching the weavers at work.

The Mohair Cottage (tel. 325430) at the Maseru Sun Cabanas has a wide variety of colourful rugs, warm blankets, illustrated tapestries and delicate shawls, and a unique range of hand-woven curtains.

Thorkild Hand Weaving (tel. 322789) is situated on the corner of Moshoeshoe and Makoanyane roads, in Maseru-West. This is one of the workshops where visitors can watch the weavers at work. There is a good selection of products which include intricate wall-hangings, carpets and stylish tablecloths.

Moteng Weavers (tel. 325380) is in a busy shop just off Moshoeshoe Road. This curio centre is popular with budget travellers: although the range is limited, this is one of the cheaper priced places on the curio route. Tapestries, wall-hangings, rugs and other traditional goods are on sale, and for any purchase over a flexible amount, a discount or free gift is included in the final price.

Being members of a livestock farming nation, who still frequently use cattle as a monetary system, the Basotho are gifted in the crafting of leather products. Exquisitely intricate handbags, shoes, belts and jackets can be bought at a number of places around the capital. Places to visit include:

Pal Products (tel. 326045) in the industrial area of Maseru.

Rose Leather Works (tel.315315) at the Bedco Centre.

Basotho Tanning (tel. 322618) on the corner of Makoanyane and Mohlomi roads.

Kabi Leather Works (tel. 313940), also located in the Bedco Centre.

The Lesotho **Save the Children Workshop** (tel. 312279) in the Bedco Centre sells leather products that are made by handicapped children in a foreign-aid programme. This is one store that sensitive travellers to Lesotho should visit. A great deal of patience, effort and commitment go into each product; the money is ploughed back into the programme to the benefit of Lesotho. Here, any querying of price or quality should be foregone in the light of what is being achieved by the Lesotho Save the Children project.

Basotho jewellery made from copper, silver, gold and semi-precious stones can be bought at any of the jewellers on Kingsway. But traditional bangles, necklaces and tribal wear are almost non-existent in Maseru. For these storytelling designs, visitors will have to travel to the remote areas of Lesotho. The natural desire of the Basotho to create art is clearly seen in their jewellery.

Royal Crown Jewellers (tel. 322318) on Caledon Road, between Maseru-West and the industrial area, has an interesting collection of products. Service is excellent, prices are high but the intricate designs are unique. One factor that should perhaps be considered by visitors, before buying from this shop, is that ivory is used in a number of the products. Given the worldwide ban on the sale of ivory and the rapidly diminishing elephant population, travellers need to question the ethics of patronising a shop that sells such products.

Seeta's Design (tel. 325887) in the LNDC Centre on Kingsway has some well crafted and reasonably priced jewellery. The large selection of earrings, rings and necklaces will have something for most shoppers. Visitors also have the option of giving the jeweller a design, choosing the metal and having the piece made while they watch.

THINGS TO SEE

Maseru being a young city by world standards there is not much of historical interest to visitors, and many of the old buildings are off limits. The major points of interest lie out of the city in the rural areas of the country.

There is a statue of Moshoeshoe the Great, first chief of the Basotho nation, in a small park south of the post office. The hill on which the new Government Complex stands was the site of Commandant

J.H. Bowker's headquarters when he came to govern Lesotho for Britain in 1869. Perhaps the most striking of all the remaining sandstone buildings is that of the Resident Commissioner built in 1891 and now housing the District Administrator's offices. Other buildings of some historical significance are the National Council Building built in 1909 and the Secretariat Building designed by Sir Herbert Baker. On the eastern side of the city, at the bus and minibus taxi depot, is Pitso Ground where many of the traditional Basotho ceremonies are performed. There is also a fascinating informal sector around Pitso Ground. About 5 km north of Maseru, from the A1 national road, a road rises towards tall radio masts and the historical site of Lancer's Gap. Here, in 1852, the ill-fated British Lancer Regiment under the command of Sir George Cathcart was defeated by Basotho warriors. From the windy summit visitors can look down across the suburbs and into the city of Maseru. Lancer's Gap is a tragic and lonely place, full of wind-songs and whispers.

Walking around the streets is still the best way of seeing Maseru. Just being among the people is an exciting experience. The Tourist Board offers city tours for visitors, as do a number of the luxury hotels. Contact the Tourist Information Centre on Kingsway (tel. 322896, fax 310108) for details of both the Maseru Explorer Tour and the longer Lesotho Adventure Tour.

6 SUGGESTED ROUTES

NORTHERN ROUTE

From MAPUTSOE – HLOTSE (LERIBE) – BUTHA BUTHE – OXBOW – MOKHOTLONG – SANI TOP
Distance: about 277 km
Road indicators: B23, A1, A14

From MAPUTSOE

Draped over a spit of land in a bend of the Caledon river, Maputsoe is a typical border town. Most shops are replicas of those in South Africa, and apart from the shanty town behind the security fence at the border, there is little of interest. Maputsoe is a transit stop for buses and minibus taxis moving migrant labour to and from the border. There is a constant stream of people crossing the Ficksburg bridge: those entering carry shopping bags and wear Western clothing, those leaving discard traditional blankets and grass hats for miner's helmets or maid's uniforms. You can expect to spend about one hour completing border formalities. Visitors with private transport, once through customs, can immediately continue into Lesotho. Those travelling in Lesotho by public transport can expect a lively reception. Buses and minibus taxis have touts who walk around cajoling and encouraging people to take their bus or taxi. Do not expect any hurry, and use the time to meet fellow passengers. Although buses in Lesotho have fixed time schedules, they seldom follow the programme and leave when the driver decides.

The Ficksburg/Maputsoe border is open 24 hours a day. The first stage in entering Lesotho is to fill in an Entry Application – have your own pen, there are never enough to go around. Once completed, the form together with passport, visa, if necessary, and vehicle ownership papers are handed in through the glass louvres to the border official. On the Entry Stamp, your date of entry and exit will be stamped. Next, your vehicle or luggage may be inspected by customs at the boom. Vehicle and luggage inspections are done randomly and are seldom thorough.

English is spoken in most shops in Maputsoe. Prices are high. There are a conspicuous number of Lesotho Traffic Officers patrolling Maputsoe, and drivers are advised to adhere to the speed limit of 50 km/h. Visitors guilty of a traffic offence have to make an immediate cash payment or a trip to the local Royal Lesotho Mounted Police for a long process of form filling and identity verification.

To leave Maputsoe, take the tarred road which runs from the border to a T-junction 6 km away. Follow the sign to Leribe and Butha Buthe.

St Monica, 4 km to the north, is perched on the edge of the Khomakoane river valley. The village has a Catholic Mission, primary school and post office. The Villa Rosa restaurant offers basic meals of porridge, mutton and beer for a few Maloti. Camping is allowed in the grounds of the mission and although no charge is made, it is good policy to give a donation when you leave. Remember that the impression you leave will affect other travellers.

From St Monica the road crosses the valley and passes the village of Tsikoane before entering Hlotse (Leribe). Between St Monica and Tsikoane are dinosaur footprints a few hundred metres from the road. These are however not very clear and visitors should travel further north for better prints.

HLOTSE (LERIBE)

The town was originally named after the Hlotse river on whose bank it lies. Although the name was later changed to Leribe, the town remains commonly known as Hlotse. Founded in 1876, Hlotse was an important town in the fierce battles of the 1880 Gun War. Hlotse is the capital of the Leribe district.

Orientation

Hlotse is 21 km from Maputsoe and lies in an east–west direction. Arriving from Maputsoe, visitors are flanked by hedges and plane trees when they enter the town. Proceed to a grass island in the road. Here signposts point the way: left to the business district of Hlotse or north towards Butha Buthe.

Those parts of Hlotse important to visitors are west of the A1 national road, near the old Anglican church, where the hotel may be found; further up around the Royal Lesotho Mounted Police Station are the post office, telephone exchange, banks and shops. To the south of town flow the muddy waters of the Hlotse river, while north the town drops to the Subeng river valley and offers views of the distant Maluti mountains. East of the national road, the town spills down a hillside before climbing to open lands dotted with goats, sheep, cattle and mud huts.

Getting around Hlotse is simple: there is only one tarred road which provides access to most sites of interest to visitors, and is the reference point from which any local exploring should begin. There are few street names visible and those are poor; they are never referred to by locals, who prefer giving directions by a vague wave of the hand in the general direction, or by naming a shop or building nearby.

Information

The post office has a telephone system to most destinations, but for international calls and poste restante it is necessary to go to the post office in Maseru. Barclays, Standard Chartered and the Lesotho Bank are located on either side of the street near the post office and the RLMP (Royal Lesotho Mounted Police). Tourist information is available from the Leribe Hotel reception desk or the District Military Commissioner's office which is situated in the RLMP building next to the radio masts.

Buses and minibus taxis arriving in and departing from Hlotse congregate in swirls of dust and exhaust fumes about 400 m south of the post office. Public transport continuing past Hlotse stops for passengers at the bus stop near the Leribe Craft Centre, at the turnoff to Katse.

Things to see

New by European standards, Hlotse does have several points of interest to visitors who are willing to spend time walking and are prepared to look beyond the litter and squalor. If arriving with your own transport, ask the police if you may park your vehicle in their grounds while you go sightseeing. Most of the officers are friendly and for the price of a few minutes' conversation are happy to guard your vehicle for a few hours.

Old Fort

Built in 1879, the British fort in Hlotse housed a garrison of colonial troops during the 1880 Gun War. Sections of the fort can still be seen in parts of Hlotse; the best preserved is the sienna-coloured tower next to the police station. Though the tower is closed (there is a rickety wooden door and iron bars), with a bit of squeezing you can poke your head inside and imagine what it must have been like to stand guard duty here – over 10 000 km and hundreds of psychic years away from Britain.

Behind the tower are the crumbling walls of the fort's prison, still with bars across the windows. A dark and dismal place, it has an eerie atmosphere and faded writing from long forgotten prisoners.

Across from the post office, a gravel road lined with pine trees leads down to the ruins of the sentries' barracks and magazine store. Resembling an old barn surrounded by a stone wall, the building is in a state of dilapidation but is still worth the visit.

Our Lady of the Name

This Anglican church, built in 1877 by English missionaries, is the oldest standing building in Hlotse. The sandstone church in its enclave of conifers could be in any English country parish – except that the nuns and congregation are mostly black and speak Sesotho. Spend a few moments drifting among the old pews in the silence and peace of the church before talking with the European nuns who have left the comforts of the First World to spend their lives helping in one of the poorest countries on earth.

Old Hlotse

Further west, behind the shops, post office and police station, is the part of Hlotse that will hold a particular fascination for travellers who have come to meet the people and share a moment of their lives. A confusion of alleys and eroded roads wind through the mixture of traditional and modern houses, each with their own little courtyard of swept earth.

The Basotho people have from early times been a pastoral nation, and this deep-rooted tradition stays with them even in towns. Most keep a few goats, chickens and cows, no matter where their houses are. This results in sights not seen in other countries. In old Hlotse there are several animal holding pens, manure heaps and communal grazing areas. Ironically, in Hlotse the Urban Improvement Sanitation Team is housed in a sandstone house behind the fort prison and in front of the local manure heap.

The most traditional part of town is on the slopes down to the Hlotse river. Mud, stone and thatch houses surrounded by low growing hedges offer meagre shelter for families that have come from remote villages in search of employment. Visitors to Hlotse will find no tourist guides in this area; it is up to you to wander among these back streets, to experience the sights and smells and meet the locals – all against a backdrop of golden coloured cliffs.

Expect to be invited into yards and houses: the friendly Basotho will want to meet you. Weekends are particularly good for seeing this side of Hlotse. The people are relaxed and happy, playing cards and games and drinking copious amounts of beer. Once you allow yourself to be invited in, the woman of the house will hurry off to prepare some "pap" (maize porridge) while the men will offer you beer and try to explain the game they are playing.

Places to stay

Unless you find a bed with a local or are willing to camp outside town, Hlotse is no bargain when it comes to tourist accommodation. There is only one hotel in town: Leribe Hotel.

Leribe Hotel (high tariff)

The hotel is on the road into the central business district across from Our Lady of the Name church. Drab and run down on the outside, the hotel is pleasantly attractive inside. The receptionists are helpful, fluent in English and able to arrange guides to the dinosaur footprints outside town. There are 33 rooms all with baths, television and comfortable beds. The tariff covers accommodation only, and meals are an "extra" charged to your account. There is a restaurant, a public and a residents' bar/lounge.
Address: Leribe Hotel, P.O. Box 14, Leribe, Lesotho
Telephone: (09266) 400362

Agricultural Training Centre (medium tariff)

Outside town, looking towards the sandstone cliffs, lies the Agricultural Training Centre, which offers accommodation to visitors if room is available. Rooms are spartan but comfortable, and guests are provided with bedding but no meals. Access to cooking facilities can be arranged by contacting the matron of the centre.

Camping (free)

If you are concerned about security around towns, approach the Red Cross Clinic, the Sisters of Charity or the Anglican church; they will allow you to camp on their property and will also supply hot water for washing and cooking. Although they expect no payment, a donation is always thankfully received.

Outside town, ask one of the old men seated in his courtyard if it is alright to camp near his house. Inevitably you will be invited inside and asked to share their home for the night, or a youngster will be assigned to watch your belongings while you talk to the adults.

Places to eat

There is only one restaurant in Hlotse of the type that Western visitors are accustomed to, at the Leribe Hotel. This is where most travellers eat and it is a good place to meet people travelling in northern Lesotho. The restaurant offers an English breakfast, à la carte lunch and set dinner. A bit expensive, meals are however well prepared, and the menu caters for most tastes, though the Basotho are not renowned vegetarians.

For the more adventurous, there are numerous eating houses scattered around town. This is where locals eat and drink and hygiene is unknown. Menus are limited but offer an excellent introduction to the Basotho staple diet of mutton and maize porridge. Once the stares of curiosity are over, people will begin to speak to you, and you will seldom be left eating alone for long. These eating houses are not signposted and it requires ingenuity to sort out the drinking houses from eating houses.

Things to buy

Good buys include mohair, woollen and grass products. In shops on the main road, most of the goods come from South Africa, but along the pavements there is a busy informal sector, where everything from traditional grass hats to fruit can be bought. On the street, bargaining is considered part of the transaction, but remember that what is mere change to you is often a loaf of bread for the vendor. Further north, on the edge of town near the turnoff to the Outward Bound School 27 km away, is the Leribe Craft Centre. Traditional Basotho products can be purchased and include woollen blankets, grass baskets and hats, beadwork and mohair jerseys. There is no bargaining at the Craft Centre and what the price tag reads is what you pay. There are Danish volunteers working at the Craft Centre, but don't expect too much communication from them: they seem to prefer ignoring foreigners.

From Hlotse, the A1 national road continues north. A road turns off it to the Lesotho Highlands Water Scheme Project at Katse, and to Pitseng and the Outward Bound School. The A1 passes the Sisters of Charity church and Red Cross Clinic before dipping to the Subeng river with its deeply eroded banks. Where the road bridges a stream, 4 km north of Hlotse, are excellent three and five-toed dinosaur footprints. These are about 400 m from the western side of the road, and the local children will show you the way for a few lisente.

The tarred road follows hill contours through forestry saplings planted in an attempt to stop erosion of the valley sides. Sandstone cliffs close to the road create gorges. About 18 km from Hlotse and 3 km from the bridge over the Mohobollo river, the road rises to Levi's Nek Pass. Not very steep or even high, the pass nevertheless gives a hint of what is to come later. At the top of the 5 km pass is a bus and minibus taxi stop, a few block houses and shops selling basic commodities and alcohol. From the summit the road plunges down Rampae's Nek Pass for 2 km to cross the Linakaleng river, and then climbs into Butha Buthe.

BUTHA BUTHE

In Sesotho, Butha Buthe means "place of security". The first stronghold of Moshoeshoe the Great, Butha Buthe was established after he had defeated the local tribes. The town is 7 km from the Caledonspoort border with South Africa, and is capital of the Butha Buthe district.

Orientation

Approximately 30 km from Hlotse, Butha Buthe sprawls in a south-north direction, with most of the suburban area being on the northern side of town below sandstone cliffs.

For visitors, relevant areas are in the western and central parts of town. The western section, left of the A1 national road which passes through Butha Buthe, is where the post office, bank buildings and RLMP (police) are found, while the central area has the hotel, mosque, open markets, craft centres, shops and – for travellers with their own transport – fuel stations. Northern and southern suburbs consist of modern residential housing.

Finding your way around Butha Buthe is easy once you have located a few distinguishing landmarks, but Lesotho's towns are most interesting when you just drift about meeting people and experiencing whatever happens, without any real sense of direction. Most towns and villages are small enough that you will never get hopelessly lost, Maseru being the exception. The sandstone cliffs to the east mark the limit of the Butha Buthe town boundary. The single tarred road through town allows access to the western suburbs by gravel roads going off at right angles.

Information

Banks are grouped together along about 1 km of dirt road, which runs west of the A1 national road. The post office and Standard Chartered are on the left side of the road, while Barclays and the modern building of the Lesotho Bank are on the right. Although a few travellers have received post at the poste restante in Butha Buthe, there is no guarantee that post will be kept for longer than three weeks, and visitors should rather have their letters sent to the post office in Maseru. Medical attention is available at the Rural Health Services Project clinic, 100 m to the west of the Crocodile Inn hotel, but expect a long wait.

Butha Buthe is arguably the easiest town in Lesotho in which to find long-distance public transport. Buses and minibus taxis have separate waiting areas. Buses arrive in and depart from the enclosed market area in the centre of town. Minibus taxis wait in ranks next to the Butha Buthe Motors garage at the southern end of town. Buses have their destinations clearly displayed, but the destinations of the minibus taxis are something of a mystery and travellers will have to ask drivers their destinations.

Things to see

Most interesting sites for visitors require some walking to be fully appreciated and understood. One attraction of exploring Butha Buthe is that the paths you follow lead through old Butha Buthe where people follow traditional customs. Without meeting the locals, visitors are in danger of missing out on the essence of Lesotho: the spirit of its people. There are reasons for its turbulent history, tightrope present and misty future, and the first step on the road to helping is getting to know the Basotho.

Within Butha Buthe, an hour's walk through the colourful streets and busy markets will bring another perspective on the Basotho culture. A good starting point is the southern end of town, along the gravel road that passes the hotel. Follow the road to the right; it continues past the green and white mosque and into the modern shopping district. Continuing north, the road ends at the tarred Caledonspoort border road (A13). Across the A13 is an intensive silviculture and plant nursery, and the foreman is delighted to show visitors around and explain the purpose of the environmentally directed project.

From the nursery, continue east into Butha Buthe, passing Roadside Spares and the abandoned Butha Buthe Hotel. At the T-junction of the A13 and A1 turn right and walk into the centre of the town. There is a mad mixture of licensed shops and pavement sellers thronging this stretch of road, and travellers will soon find themselves caught up in the excitement of the people as they bargain, shout, laugh and argue their way through the chaos.

Moshoeshoe's first mountain stronghold

Butha Buthe's main attraction for visitors is the mountain fortress of Moshoeshoe the Great. On the towering sandstone cliffs overlooking northern Butha Buthe, Lesotho's first king initially settled with his tribesmen, wives, children and livestock.

The climb to the top is strenuous and people are advised to carry waterbottles and rest frequently on the steep hillside. From the turnoff to the Caledonspoort border post, go east past the big yellow "Build Rite Bricks" sign and follow the path which climbs past houses with large vegetable gardens. At the top of this small hill, take the left path which skirts a dairy and continues to a T-junction where a sand road intersects the path. Turn right along the road to where it ends at the river. Cross the shallow water and walk into the glade surrounded by fragrant Eucalyptus trees. A small waterfall tumbles at the eastern end of the glade, and apart from the sighs of the wind in the trees and the sound of running water, the place is silent and peaceful. Cross to the far tree-lined bank and up into the cultivated lands, below the base of the mountain. Continue east as far as the water pipe that runs from the summit. Follow the stony trail to the left of the pipe, then a steep climb for 300 m to the top.

Trees have been planted on the summit to prevent soil erosion and enhance the mystery of the site. From the western edge of the summit plateau, a spectacular view is afforded of Butha Buthe below. There is a strange atmosphere on the mountain and some visitors are convinced they hear voices in the long grass and among the stones. After the frantic streets of Butha Buthe, the mountain fortress is a calm haven swept clean by the winds from the distant Maluti mountains.

Sekubu caves and dinosaur footprints

On the road north, 7 km from the bus depot in Butha Buthe, is a turnoff to the right, signposted "Sekubu," which lies 9 km east. The settlement is touristy, with would-be guides jumping out to offer their services as soon as you arrive.

The shallow sandstone caves are intriguing in that they were once inhabited by bushmen long before Moshoeshoe arrived as conqueror. Local legends tell of the "little people" who once lived in the area, hunted with bow and arrows and painted stories on the walls of their cave homes.

Faint dinosaur footprints can be seen, and the location is a step back in time. Try to arrive in the late afternoon when the sun splashes the surrounding cliffs with liquid gold and adds to the ethereal mood of the place, suspending, for an instant, the chasm of ages.

Places to stay

Accommodation in Butha Buthe is limited, and the densely populated countryside makes camping a security risk. There is only one hotel in town, but camping and basic accommodation are available at the Youth Hostel.

Crocodile Inn (high tariff)

Located in the southern suburbs of Butha Buthe, the Crocodile Inn is 200 m up the gravel road west of Butha Buthe Motors, and is well signposted. The hotel is comfortable and well placed for trips to the surrounding areas. Its quiet grounds and empty swimming pool hint at another era.

The present owner-manager, Stuart Henderson, is a mine of information on the area and has an abundance of anecdotes gleaned from his years in Lesotho; some amusing, others sad, all tinged with self-scrutiny. Like most men who have chosen to make their life in Africa, he is likeable and easygoing, with an eye for detail that has his hotel recommended by the Lesotho Tourist Board.

There are 25 rooms; 20 have baths, the other five have showers. The showers have low pressure but are fitted with attachments that provide hot water when you turn on either of the taps in the basin while showering. All rooms have television and receive programmes from South Africa and channel TV. The tariff includes both bed and breakfast but excludes lunch and dinner, which are available from the dining room. There is a snooker room and residents' bar with gambling machines (slot machines). Outside, a large hall serves as a public bar and television lounge for non-residents.

Camping is permissible at the hotel, but the facilities are not really adequate and apart from the camping fee, additional charges are made for the use of hot water.

Address: Crocodile Inn, P.O. Box 72, Butha Buthe, Lesotho
Telephone: (09266) 460223

Youth Hostel (medium tariff)

About 4 km out of Butha Buthe, near St Paul's Mission, the Youth Hostel is well situated for visitors hoping to see a church mission in rural Africa. There is an office of the Youth Hostel in Butha Buthe, from where transport can be arranged for people without their own vehicles. The office is in the B.B. Jersey and Woollen Factory, on the corner of the A13 from the Caledonspoort border and the A1 running through Butha Buthe. Open from Monday to Friday 09h00–16h30, the office is closed on Saturdays and Sundays (and usually after 12h00 on Fridays).

There are 16 beds in separate rooms for men and women, but the warden is willing to let couples share if the hostel is empty.

It is necessary to provide your own food, which can be bought in Butha Buthe before you go to the hostel. Cooking stoves, cutlery and crockery are kept in the kitchen and may be used by guests. Washing and ablution facilities are communal. (A hygiene tip: take a pair of cheap plastic sandals along which you can wear while showering.) During winter there is insufficient bedding available and travellers should take sleeping bags or a sheet to line the mattress. A discount of 3% is offered to visitors who have an International Youth Hostel Federation card – these are available through travel agents and student bodies in most countries.

Address: P.O. Box 96, Butha Buthe, Lesotho
Telephone: (09266) 460306

Places to eat

Butha Buthe has numerous fast-food places on either side of the A1 road, but they can be overcrowded and you can expect a long wait before your order is filled. A good idea is to place your order and then go for a walk along the bustling main street of Butha Buthe. The advantage of these take-away shops is that they have good food at reasonable prices and are clean. Tony's Fast Foods, in the old sandstone building near the bus depot, is popular and does a variety of excellent snacks both Western and local.

Given the unofficial eating houses and street vendors, the visitor is unlikely to go hungry while exploring Butha Buthe. Street vendors, who line the western side of the A1 national road through Butha Buthe, roast corn on the cob over wood fires, bake heavy but delicious brown bread and sell fruit and vegetables. Meanwhile, in the tin-shack eating houses scattered around town, the diet is basic but satisfying.

At the Crocodile Inn, a small dining room offers à la carte lunch, dinner and breakfast; it is a little expensive but is comfortable and cool, and the food and service are of a high standard. Visitors not staying at the inn should book a few hours ahead, especially over weekends and public holidays.

Things to buy

A good selection of traditional Basotho handicrafts is available in Butha Buthe. These can be haggled over in the open markets or on the streets, or considered in the shops recognised by the Tourist Board, which are more expensive. Butha Buthe has a reputation for fine knitwear, which was first introduced to Lesotho by the colonising British in the late 1800s. The conical-shaped hat shop at the northern end of the business district houses the B.B. Jersey and Woollen Factory, and also the Youth Hostel office. Patterned mohair and woollen jerseys are on sale, as well as colourful scarves, carpets and shawls.

North of Butha Buthe the road drops away from town, following the base of Moshoeshoe's mountain fortress through flat countryside. In the distance, to the north and east, rise the peaks of the Maluti mountains. This is the start of the famous Roof of Africa road, where rally drivers test their skills over some of the highest and worst roads in Africa.

Visitors with their own transport should note that it is about 60 km to the next available fuel at Oxbow Lodge, and it is advisable to fill tanks in Butha Buthe. The tarred road climbs up into rarefied air. Fuel consumption is high on this low-gear section of the northern route.

Once out of Butha Buthe, the road passes through agricultural lands. During late summer this area is a sea of ripe sorghum and maize, and the road is lined with flowering cosmos. To the east, across the valley from the A1, centuries of wind and water erosion have sculptured amazing shapes in the soft sandstone cliffs. It is pleasant to walk among these cliffs, listening to the songs of the wind and looking across the thatched villages in the shallow valley below.

As the road rises out of the lowlands of Lesotho, the modern block and tin houses are replaced by villages built in circular fashion, with stone walls and thatched roofs. About 14 km from Butha Buthe the village of Ha Marakabei straddles the national road and has poor accommodation in the Cindi Lodge. Apart from a short bus stop or breakdown, there is no reason to stop in Ha Marakabei, and most travellers pass through and into the steep valleys of the Hololo river.

Next comes the village of Khukhune, marked by a store and a sign proclaiming a combined Ireland/Lesotho Rural Development Project. For people desperate to stay at Khukhune, a tin shanty is available at a low price, and consists of a bed-stand, sand floor and bucket of cold water. Unless you are protected by insect repellent and antiseptic, this accommodation is not recommended. North of the village the Khukhune river (1 643 m) is crossed and the road starts to become challenging.

At this stage most travellers begin to realise that the sides of the valley are closing in on the road. Over the Ngoe river the road rises in a series of bends before dropping to the Malefiloane river and the Riverside General Café at 1 831 m.

At 27 km from Butha Buthe, the Moteng Lodge nestles at the base of the steepest part of the road to Oxbow. This is also the last stop before Oxbow for buses travelling from the south. No fuel is available, but there is a "tuck shop" stocked with tinned foods, cooldrinks, crisps and sometimes bread. Moteng Lodge falls into the medium tariff category and is seldom used in the summer and autumn, but during winter, when it snows, it is impossible to find accommodation here. Given the unreliable postal and telephone service in this region, the accommodation is awarded on a first-come-first-served basis. There are 10 rooms, each with bathroom and either one or two beds. À la carte menus are offered for lunch and dinner, and an English breakfast is served.

North of Moteng Lodge the first major climb on the northern route commences. With a 5,5 km section of 19% gradient the road twists and turns around hairpin bends, past gossamer waterfalls and up towards the summit. Signs warn of rock falls, and sections of the road are littered with boulders. Regularly each year, melting snow and rain wash tonnes of rocks and soil onto the road, blocking the pass until heavy machinery can be brought up to clear the road.

Yet, despite the dangers, once you have arrived at the summit of the Moteng Pass (2 810 m), the view is reward enough. A view-point has been provided for visitors. There is nothing but loneliness and the damp wind on the summit. To the south, the lowlands are faintly visible through the rising heat of the plains; to the north and east rise mountain ranges. Often the jingle of a cowbell can be heard, but already there are fewer people and the countryside is wilder and more remote.

From the top of the pass the road skirts a mountain in a gentle downhill to the Hydrological, Wireless and First Aid Station above the Tsehlanyane river (2 595 m). Another view-point is provided on the eastern side of the 13% gradient sign. Again the views are spectacular and in late summer the view-point is carpeted with wild flowers growing in the Alpine silence. A steep downhill levels out on the valley floor and the road enters Oxbow.

OXBOW

Oxbow is not a town or even a village: a single building, the New Oxbow Lodge, is all that makes up the place.

New Oxbow Lodge (high tariff)

Popular during winter, the Oxbow Lodge is a mecca for South African skiers. The surrounding slopes are regularly covered in blankets of powdery snow, offering some of the best skiing on the continent. The lodge is perched over the icy waters of the Malibatmatso river (3 000 m). The owner has created a ski-lodge atmosphere. In winter a roaring fire warms the well-stocked bar, whose walls are lined with skiing photographs and amusing anecdotes.

Accommodation is in 24 rooms all with bathroom and clean linen. Surprisingly, the tariff includes both bed and breakfast. Lunch and dinner can be chosen from a small menu in the Swiss styled dining room at an expensive price. Oxbow Lodge is secluded in a steep-sided valley in one of the few regions on earth where there are no fences.

Horseriding, hiking and trout-fishing are all available, and the owner should be contacted for arrangements. Because the lodge is popular, visitors are advised to make reservations several weeks in advance, especially during winter. Take sufficient warm clothing; an extra blanket or sleeping bag is useful in winter. This is the last place where a guaranteed supply of fuel is available before Mokhotlong, nearly 114 km away to the east.

Buses travelling the A1 use the lodge as a refreshment stop. For budget travellers, the owner is willing to allow camping on the front lawn, and charges a small fee for use of hot showers. One problem often encountered by campers is the attentions of the territorial geese and raucous turkey which compete for space on the lawn. But once a peace offering is made with crusts of bread or fruit, they waddle off before returning in the early evening to sleep in their coop. (Imagine if someone suddenly pitched a tent on your front lawn without asking?)

Address: New Oxbow Lodge, P.O. Box 43, Maputsoe, Lesotho
Telephone: (05192) 2247 (South Africa)

A mere 500 m further north the tar ends, the road crosses a bridge and rises onto the highest drivable road in Africa. This is where the adventure that is northern Lesotho begins. No two travellers share the same experiences along this road, but all agree that the friendliness and hospitality of the mountain people are unrivalled in Lesotho.

The level road winds through a series of low hills until rising to a steep-sided plateau. Most of the scenery is austere and brown, with hills covered in grey heather. Just 13 km from the end of the tar, three stone shepherd's huts stand about 100 m from the road on a narrow spur above a deep valley. Though unable to speak English, the young shepherds, with their packs of mongrel dogs, are delighted to see visitors. They will offer you a meal of goat-milk and porridge, and pose for photos with their flocks.

At the end of the Fanana valley, about 17 km from Oxbow, lies the Maluti Ski-Club. No accommodation is available for non-members, but there are facilities for club members. Skiing can be arranged for non-members via the Oxbow Lodge, including skiing equipment and transport to the slopes. The ski area is a few kilometres further on up the slopes, which roll down to the Oxbow–Mokhotlong road.

From the valley the road rises for 10 km up to the Mahlasela Pass (3 230 m). Below the pass lies the Motete valley, framed by towering peaks and windswept dales. Visitors will notice that there are no fences in this wilderness and lands are marked by stone cairns that stand as silent sentries along the ridges of the mountains. From a distance these cairns look like blanketed shepherds, and that apparently is the intention.

A number of potholed bends twist down for 8 km to the banks of the Motete river. Few people inhabit this region, and apart from shepherds and remote villages far from the road, travellers are alone in this pristine wilderness. At a height of 3 240 m the road crests a hill at the Pass of the Guns. The old bridle path from Mont-aux-Sources can be seen making its tortuous way through the steep valley.

Another 5 km south the road emerges on the summit of the highest road pass in Africa: Tlaeeng Pass (3 275 m). The sensation of being on the roof of Africa is dramatic. In all directions, mountains lie below you, and to the south are the disused diamond diggings, like an open sore, at Mothae. The wind howls around the signboard and most people hurry down towards the stone village in the valley, to the east of the open-cast diamond mines. This village, once part of the Letseng-la-Terae diamond mine, is a study in poverty. Built of sandstone, plastic and tin, the village huddles among rusted engines and torn hillsides; an icy wind constantly rushes through the valley. The people however have risen above their surroundings, and visitors are greeted with smiles and handshakes.

It is too easy to remain aloof from these villages. Visitors speed past in the insulation of 4x4s, not experiencing even a hint of the life that the locals must endure. It costs nothing to stop and walk through this mining village in the depths of the Maluti. No matter how immune a person may be to the suffering of others, the curious stares of the naked children, the tattered thin blankets of the old people and the laughing faces but sad eyes of the adults will affect all who take the trouble to visit this mountain wilderness. In summer and autumn the village is carpeted in wild flowers and the ugliness of the disused machinery is hidden for a few glorious months. The village chief lives in the big stone house with yellow plastic curtains, across from the diesel tanks. Although he speaks little English, he is willing to let you camp anywhere around the village. The buses travelling between Oxbow and Mokhotlong will stop for a few minutes so that you can walk through the village, and the driver will hoot loudly when it is time to go. Most of the mining area is forbidden to visitors, but once you are over the hill behind the fenced transport yard, no-one will bother you as you wander around the empty diggings.

South from the village at Letseng-la-Terae, the road climbs to the district boundary between Butha Buthe and Mokhotlong. According to the chief in Letseng-la-Terae, there was a signpost at the boundary a long time ago, but now the site is marked by two stone cairns and the silence. From the pass it is 23 km further to Mopholaneng village on the Khubelu river. This is one of the most isolated regions of Lesotho and the lack of contact with outsiders causes the people to be interested and excited when visitors stop. Mopholaneng is a dusty little village that could provide an excellent base for hikers exploring the valleys in the region. The village is relaxed and easygoing and travellers often comment on the peace that warms the village.

A small village lies 2 km further south across the river. At the foot of the village are caves with faint paintings by the long-gone Bushmen[1] who once lived in these mountains.

Arriving at the top of the next section of road, travellers will immediately notice the enormous Tlokoeng sign painted in white on a red roof across the valley. Follow the road towards the dam in the valley. About 200 m beyond the dam is a village which has signposts indicating the way to Tlokoeng and Ha Meta, or straight on towards Mokhotlong. There is a small airfield at Tlokoeng and the largest store in the area, established in 1926 by Kenneth Nolan. Fuel has not been regularly available at Tlokoeng for many years, but recently a supply has occasionally been brought in, and visitors in their own vehicles are sometimes fortunate enough to find some.

About 4 km south on the road to Mokhotlong, on the eastern side of the valley, is a high cliff. Stout-hearted visitors can make an exciting and dangerous walk to the caves in this cliff. Walk down from the main road to the river. A green bridge, built by overseas volunteers, crosses the river to the north of the cliff. Cross the bridge and follow the path that goes up towards the village. After about 200 m turn right and cross the spur of land to come out above the cliff. Walk along the top of the cliff until you come to a gulley and a ledge that leads around the cliffside and out onto the wall. The narrow ledge, about a metre wide, crosses the face of the cliff and provides a wonderful opportunity to look into the cracks and caves that fissure the cliff. The locals in the village say that the caves were once used as burial tombs and have paintings in them. I spent well over two hours shuffling back and forth along the ledge and, apart from a few hyrax skeletons, found nothing.

1 While the generic term "Bushman" is used throughout the book when referring to rock paintings, readers should note that there is considerable argument concerning the original rock painters of Lesotho – whether they were of the Khoikhoi or San tribes. To eliminate any distinction between the two, "Bushman" has been used.

Another 5 km south the road drops to cross the Senqu river, then winds up to the T-junction that branches east to Mokhotlong, or south along the Drakensberg road to Sani Top and the border. One kilometre along the road to Mokhotlong are a police post and stone-walled sale yards. Every Tuesday a stock sale is held – a fascinating event to attend. The Basotho men, in blankets, gumboots and woollen caps, bring their stock down from the villages in large groups. Ponies, cattle, sheep and goats are penned in the walled area and the owners retire for a drink before the sale begins. Prospective buyers jump into the mud-filled pen and examine the animals for soundness. This lasts for about two hours, after which another period of liquid refreshment is taken. Then one of the men dressed in a blanket, city-shoes and sunglasses gets up and starts the sale. Don't even try to follow what is going on; a stock sale here bears little resemblance to any Western stock sale. Amid continual shouting, pushing, shoving and raising of sticks the animals are sold. Once about half the animals have been offered, more beer is drunk; then the selling continues until all the stock has been offered or the people lose interest and wander off home or for more beer. For a visitor merely to see such a stock sale, and spend a few hours mixing with the stockmen, means to have touched the real face of northern Lesotho.

To the east, 10 km away, the road gradually descends to the town of Mokhotlong, 182 km from Butha Buthe.

MOKHOTLONG

Meaning "place of the bald ibis," Mokhotlong is a town with a frontier atmosphere. The first and last major town before the difficult Sani Pass, it has a steady stream of traffic from the mountain roads. Mokhotlong lies cradled in a bowl formed by the winding Mokhotlong river, is frequently cut off in the snows of winter and offers visitors a magical alpine setting. In spite of its status as the district capital, Mokhotlong has the reputation of being the remotest town in Lesotho.

Orientation

Arriving from the A1, travellers take a gravel road around a number of hills before descending to the town, which stretches in an east-west direction. Although the main part of Mokhotlong lies along a 2 km section of road, suburbs spread over a wide expanse of valley and across the Mokhotlong river to the north, and continue up a terraced hillside to the south.

Relevant parts of Mokhotlong include the 2 km of road about 150 m east of the waterpump. This section of road is untarred and severely damaged, but is lined by shops, the bank, post office, RLMP (police) and eating and drinking houses. To the north of the town, beyond the airport and school, the Mokhotlong river flows in a series of bends. The eastern end of Mokhotlong is still traditional, while the western end is marked by modern block houses.

Finding your way in Mokhotlong is simple. The town lies in a hollow of the surrounding valley floor. So, to get your bearings look either up along the hillsides or down into Mokhotlong.

Information

Tourist information is available at the Senqu Hotel or, if you don't mind the wait, at the Military District Commissioner's office in the RLMP building next to the post office.

According to the postal workers, nobody has ever tried to use the post office as a poste restante and apart from correspondence for the businesses located in the area, very little post arrives in Mokhotlong. The Lesotho Bank is fenced in behind a row of Lombardy poplars and is across from the only fuel point in town. East of the Lesotho Bank, a road goes down to the airport, which is about 1 km from town.

Public transport from Mokhotlong stops near the Lesotho Electricity Corporation next to the Lesotho Bank. Drivers will, however, stop anywhere from the entrance sign to Mokhotlong as far as the turning circle 100 m north of the Mokhotlong Hotel. Ask at the RLMP station for expected times of departure.

Things to see

For visitors who have travelled to Lesotho to see typical tourist sites, Mokhotlong has nothing to offer. But those who travel for the same reasons as Robert Louis Stevenson, who said, "I travel not to go anywhere, but simply to go," will find Mokhotlong an exciting and captivating town. The best way to see Mokhotlong is to leave your transport at one of the hotels and walk.

Start a walk from the western end of Mokhotlong, just below the new block houses on the western hillside. The sandy road is often curtained in clouds of dust as the wind from the Drakensberg mountains further east scours the valley. When this happens, wear a scarf around your face and seek refuge in one of the shanty cafés or bars that are everywhere in Mokhotlong. The first cluster of buildings provides an interesting mixture of new and old, with a modern beer-hall, butchery and hair salon surrounded by traditional stone huts. The steps of the beer-hall are a good place to sit watching people go about their business of living. Across, at the waterpump, young women fill gourds and plastic containers with water for cooking and cleaning. There is always a crowd gathered at the pump and the people are friendly, if somewhat curious about foreigners walking among them.

East of the beer-hall is a stream which is also the local laundry site. On Mondays and Thursdays groups of women, with babies strapped to their backs, go there with bundles of washing. They scrub and beat their clothes and blankets with smooth pebbles and hard green soap, then hang the washing out to dry on any available strand of wire. Most of them are at first shy and selfconscious, but soon start to talk and laugh once their uncertainty has passed.

The road then climbs a short hill and passes the Mokhotlong sign into the main street. This street is a jumble of buildings and street stalls, with lots of people milling about or shopping. At the bar marked "Castle Milkstout," men leave their horses in rows outside while they play cards and carouse inside. No Western movie could be more real than this. You may be approached by beggars, mostly children, but do not encourage them: adult Basothos are often embarrassed by this and will frequently chase these children away. Continue walking along the main road, stopping to look at things for sale at the street stalls. Be careful of the traffic that congests the central area of Mokhotlong. Speed limits in town are ignored and drivers speed along the potholed road – on either side!

Expect to be stared at as you walk the streets; it is uncommon for foreigners to spend time exploring Mokhotlong. The simple answer is to smile. The Basotho are a happy nation, quick to laugh and joke, and they appreciate the same in outsiders, even if communication is difficult.

Along the Mokhotlong river to the north of Mokhotlong are several caves with good paintings and what looks like the ruins of old villages. If you are venturing out towards this side of Mokhotlong, it is advisable to take along a day-pack, some warm clothing and food. Although the cliffs, valleys and caves are only about 2 km away, the weather in and around Mokhotlong is unpredictable. Sudden storms and mist can hide the town within minutes, and a basic knowledge of weather forecasting would be an advantage for those planning to camp, travel or hike in this district. Some visitors may experience headaches and shortness of breath. This is usually due to the high altitude, and apart from spending a few days in the area, there is little that can be done, except taking a headache tablet or sleeping for a few hours.

Take the path that skirts the river at the eastern end of Mokhotlong; it follows a stream which eventually spills into the cold waters of the Mokhotlong river. The path passes huts and cultivated plots where locals are amusingly surprised to see foreigners walking past their back gardens. On reaching the Mokhotlong river, travellers can either walk along the western bank through the groves of trees or turn east to cross the bridge further up the valley. To the north of the river, cliffs rise from the riverbank and are bathed in soft light during the late afternoon. There are many caves to be investigated in and around these cliffs, some featuring in legends of ancient peoples and tribal rites. Children offer their services from the little hamlet on the river, below the Mokhotlong airport. These youngsters can often save you a lot of time by leading you straight to the sites. Alternatively visitors can go alone, with only their spirit of adventure and urge to explore as their guides. Whichever way you choose, it is safer to start this walk early and return to Mokhotlong before sunset. Darkness comes quickly, and the prospect of spending a night on the exposed mountains usually hurries most visitors back to town. Sometimes people from the hotels who have gone on this walk do stay out after dark, but the hotel staff are quick to notify the RLMP (police) who, once having found the missing people, are not averse to having them spend the rest of the night in the local jail.

Places to stay

Mokhotlong is the only town along the northern route that is graced by two hotels: the Senqu Hotel and Mokhotlong Hotel. Camping is not a problem, though security can be if you camp near the shanties at the north-eastern edge of the town.

Senqu Hotel (high tariff)

The hotel, painted orange, is on the left side of the road as it enters the western suburbs of Mokhotlong. The Senqu is the better of the two hotels in Mokhotlong. With dark corridors and an absence of light bulbs, the Senqu offers visitors peace and privacy. The manager is helpful, fluent in English and friendly, with a good knowledge of the region. If requested, pony-treks to the valleys or a guide for hikes to the higher peaks in the area can be arranged.

There are 10 rooms all with bath and either one, two or three beds. The rooms are clean with carpeted floors, guest soap and white towels. A tastefully decorated dining room is available to guests, as are a lounge, television and video room and small residents' bar. Outside there is ample parking, a public bar and 24-hour security. The tariff covers room only; meals are an additional expense. The hotel seldom has foreign guests and the effort to make your stay as pleasant as possible is obvious.

Address: Senqu Hotel, P.O. Box 23, Mokhotlong, Lesotho
Telephone: (09266) 920330

Mokhotlong Hotel (high tariff)

At the eastern end of the main road through Mokhotlong, on the edge of a stream and shielded from the wind by a stand of plane trees, the Mokhotlong Hotel is drab, grey and poorly kept. Originally the only hotel in town, the Mokhotlong was established by a local trader who would take donkey trains down the Sani Pass to South Africa for supplies. The heyday of the hotel is over and only a token staff is in attendance. There is no allocated parking and visitors should not expect good service.

There are 10 rooms all with bath, one or two beds and a dressing table. Most of the rooms are in a state of disrepair and many of the windows cannot be closed. In the entrance hall is a television which is viewed by most of the neighbours who crowd onto the three-seater couch and the floor. The tariff includes room only and although meals can be arranged it seems to be a lot of trouble. If you decide to stay at the Mokhotlong Hotel take along food which can be cooked on the stoves in the hotel kitchen. No soap or towels are available for guests and visitors are advised to take along insect spray.

The receptionist is able to arrange pony-rides and guides for visitors wanting to explore Mokhotlong and further north, as far up as the headwaters of the Bafali river, a tributary of the Mokhotlong river.

Address: Mokhotlong Hotel, P.O. Box 13, Mokhotlong, Lesotho

Camping (free)

The hills and valleys around Mokhotlong offer campers many opportunities. It is best to avoid the fringe areas of the town for security reasons. From the bus stop near the FMU building, follow the road leading north towards the airport. About 1 km further the road becomes a path that leads down to the Mokhotlong river. The strip of bank gets wider 200 m downstream, and there are level sections of land higher up the hill that offer safety should the river flood in the night – a real threat in this area.

Avoid drinking water from the Mokhotlong river as it has numerous tributaries passing through Mokhotlong, which are used for disposal and washing purposes. Campers can expect a few curious children initially, but after a while they leave you alone until the next morning.

Higher up the valleys, ask the chief of the nearest settlement for permission to camp in his territory. You may even be offered a hut for the night, which is an experience not to be missed.

Places to eat

Mokhotlong being the travellers' stop that it is, has a bewildering number of places offering food. Items range from full à la carte menus to a piece of brown bread and a hot peppery sauce.

Top of the range is the dining room of the Senqu Hotel. Reservations are necessary even though the place is seldom busy. Most of the diners are civil servants and businessmen who speak in hushed whispers or not at all. The menu is à la carte and moderately priced, with a wide range of meals, from soup, fish and poultry to steaks, salads and sweets. Each order is specially prepared and you need to sit back and relax while you wait. If you find yourself eating at the Senqu Hotel on a full-moon night, listen for the sounds of drums which echo down the valleys. It takes a great deal of self-control not to let your imagination run riot.

For visitors wanting to mix with the locals, there are many eating and drinking houses. Apart from small scribbled signs above their doors, there is little to guide you. In most of the alleys running off the main road, there is at least one eating establishment. Those behind the shops at the waterpump offer a standard meal of mutton or goat and porridge. Though the meal is simple there is no charge for second helpings and the company is always interesting. The café to the left of the beer-hall (up the short path and into a stone hut) serves large portions of traditional food at low prices.

Street vendors along the road through Mokhotlong offer excellent snacks, fruit and vegetables. Buy some of the heavy brown bread which is sold in pieces from a large circular loaf. This bread, together with tomato, onions and a mug of tea, makes a satisfying meal. Other foods on sale from the street vendors are mutton boiled in an evil-looking sauce, roasted corn on the cob, various goat stews and loads of organically grown vegetables.

Things to buy

Mokhotlong has little to offer in the way of curios, but there are some traditional items available. At the MKG Wool Centre, in the narrow alley next to the stall of the "sangoma" (medicine man), shoppers will find rolls of dyed wool. The wool is shorn from the flocks which spend summer grazing in the high meadows of northern Lesotho. The shop-assistant also has a number of locally knitted jerseys in undyed black, grey and white wool. Very few of the locals wear the conical grass hats of their countrymen further south: the climate is too cold and wet for grass crafts.

Various assortments of trinkets are sold by the street vendors and range from pink sunglasses to paper shopping bags. Remember that bargaining is expected, and have loose cash, as vendors never seem able to find the correct amount of change for large denominations.

There are also the more conventional shops whose shelves are stocked with products a lot cheaper across the nearby border in South Africa. One peculiarity that might interest tea drinkers is that the strongly flavoured and refreshing Zimbabwean tea, Tanganda, is sold at Gany's Supermarket below the Mokhotlong Egg Circle building. How this tea came to be available in a dark and cluttered shop in the mountains of northern Lesotho – while hardly ever being found outside Zimbabwe – is a mystery the owner was not prepared to clarify.

Mokhotlong does not have any one attraction, but the atmosphere, scenery and smiling hill-people make it one of the most interesting towns in Lesotho. A little off the beaten track, it offers adventure, excitement and a chance to experience what the locals mean when they say,"You cannot be refreshed and not smile."

At the beginning of the twentieth century there were few foreigners who had ever travelled the Drakensberg road from Mokhotlong to Sani Pass. It remained unseen, unvisited, shrouded in mist on the roof of Africa. A sense of mystery still clings to this mountain route, partly because it was for so long inaccessible, partly because the mountains, valleys and remote villages of this region never really gave up all their secrets, have never become commonplace or spoiled by package tours and travel magazines.

At the T-junction on the A1, the road also branches right, to Sani Top, Thaba Tseka and St James. There is no public transport to Sani Top and travellers will have to hitch there from Mokhotlong. Walk about 500 m along the road, south from the turnoff, and flag down a vehicle heading east. Most vehicles will stop, and it is a good idea to accept the ride however far the driver is going. For visitors with their own transport, fill up with fuel in Mokhotlong and expect to drive over what is probably the worst road in Lesotho. The trip takes about two hours to the chalet at Sani Top.

The road dips towards a deep valley, skirts a village and then crosses a stream. At the top of the hill is the sign pointing the way to St James Mission, whose buildings can be seen over the hills to the south.

Camping is allowed at the mission and the nuns, French-Canadian Sisters of Saint Joseph of the Hyacinth, are friendly and jovial, with a gentleness and tranquillity in contrast to the harshness and violence of the wild countryside. They offer a glade of willow and plane trees below the stone dining room, and will give you two buckets of boiling water for washing and cooking. The young student nuns often walk down to visit campers and their scrubbed moon faces are smothered in smiles and joy. The church is built in the shape of a large cross and it is interesting to sit in one of the pews and look at the pictures that the local congregation have painted on the ceilings and walls. Though no fee is asked for camping, a contribution is thankfully accepted and goes a long way in easing what can only be described as a hard and trying life.

Walk up the hill that rises from the road above the mission. There is a spectacular view over the mission, surrounding hills and across to the peaks of the Drakensberg.

Following the A14 south-east, visitors will find themselves in the valley of the Sakeng river. The hills are heather-covered and steep, frequented only by sheep and goats which nibble the green grass hidden below the grey heather. Hills close in and the slope side of the road is blocked by volcanic cliffs, while the river side becomes a vertical drop to the turbulent river. This is the hidden country of Lesotho, the beautiful region between the Maluti and Drakensberg mountains. It is an area that needs protection from the depredations of the time-conscious modern world, a place of silence and natural beauty.

About 26 km from Mokhotlong the road crosses the Kotisephola Pass (Black Mountain, 3 240 m). There is no sign to indicate the pass, but the poles that once held the sign are still there, whistling a sorrowful tune in the wind. There are magnificent views in all directions from the summit of the pass, and to the north-east is the highest mountain in southern Africa, Thabana-Ntlenyana (3 482 m). This is a good place to stop after the drive up from the valleys of the Sakeng and Sehonglag rivers, and before the difficult descent to the Sani Flats. This is surely one of the last surviving storehouses of human wholeness, a mountain wilderness of sanity, a place where the soul is revealed, chastened and inspired all at the same time.

Dropping steeply from the Kotisephola Pass, the road deteriorates into a track littered with stones, boulders, rusting vehicle bodies and dangerous corners. This road is definitely unsuitable for cars, and visitors planning to travel this route should do it in a 4x4, motorbike or mountain bike (though pedalling a bicycle would be strenuous in the thin mountain air). It is a 3 km descent to the wide floor of the Sani Flats, but these few kilometres will take the longest time on the drive from Mokhotlong to Sani Top.

Below the hills, the valley opens out into a wide undulating plain which ends in cliffs that plunge into South Africa. A few villages lie scattered about the flats, but the people are shy and strangely suspicious of tourists. Covered in snow during winter and early spring, the Sani Flats are a mass of colour during summer and autumn: fields of white and pink Rhodohypoxis flowers interspersed with the soft grey and bright yellow of Crassula plants. At the eastern end of the flats is the Lesotho border post, with the South African border 8 km away, down the Sani Pass.

SANI TOP

To the left of the border as one comes from Mokhotlong, there is a dirt track that passes the settlement of Sani Top and goes to the Sani Top Chalet, which is perched on the edge of a cliff above the awesome Sani Pass. The chalet, which falls into the medium tariff category, has eight rooms and 24 beds. Visitors are expected to provide their own food, but cooking facilities are available. If the chalet is full, which is usually the case over weekends and during winter, camping is permitted and a nominal fee charged if the kitchen and residents' bar are used. Clean bedding is provided and the residents' bar is open all day over weekends and every evening. A panorama window looks out over the highlands of South Africa and provides an ideal place for spotting birds that live on the cliffs below the chalet. A pamphlet, "Guide to the birds of South Africa," is provided and a pair of binoculars would be useful.

For guests wanting to explore some of the rugged area around Sani Top, the chalet housekeeper can arrange ponies or guides with a few hours' notice. This region is a wonderland for nature enthusiasts, and a short walk in any direction leads to points offering awesome views. There is little to disturb the tranquillity of the surrounding hills, and the sounds that do reach your ears are of cow bells, bird calls and the occasional far-away echo of a vehicle slowly climbing the twists and turns of the pass. Walkers should be careful of the mist which rises from the lower valleys and can quickly blanket the whole of Sani Top. The chalet can be chilly, and visitors end up sitting in the cheerfully decorated dining room, huddled around the coal stove. A definite bonus, after hours of walking or arduous driving from South Africa or Mokhotlong, is the hot shower available at the chalet. Electricity comes from a generator which is shut down at 20h30; guests are then given paraffin lamps which cast weird shadows on the white walls of the rooms. The Sani Top Chalet is very popular. As one guest from Denmark wrote in the visitors' book, "This is what the gateway of heaven must look like." Reservations over weekends and during the snow season are necessary; book at least one month in advance. Skiing and sledging equipment is available at the chalet, and a trip can be organised for a day's walk to the top of Thabana-Ntlenyana. There is a public bar with television in the stone building across from the chalet entrance.

Address: c/o Himeville Arms Hotel, P.O. Box 105, Himeville 4583, South Africa.

Telephone: South Africa 033722 – ask for number 5.

To the west is the village of Sani Top where a few basic supplies are available at a small store. Most of the villagers are related to the border police, and as is typical of places where tourists are regular, there is a lot of begging from the children – which is not to be encouraged. There are a number of planned changes to the area; one is the construction of a hiker's hut to the south of the border post, which is also the end of the Top-of-the-Berg walk from the Sehlabathebe National Park 40 km away. The border crossing, where visitors must report for their entrance or exit stamps, is 100 m away.

CENTRAL ROUTE

From HLOTSE – LEJONE – THABA TSEKA – MARAKABEI – ROMA – SEMONKONG – THABA BOSIU – TEYATEYANENG
Distance: about 730 km
Road indicators: B25, A3, A5, B21, A1

From HLOTSE

Across from the Leribe Craft Centre, a tarred road turns east towards the highlands of central Lesotho. The sign indicates: Katse, Thaba Tseka and Outward Bound School. One kilometre further on, across from the Lesotho Electricity Commission, is a path going up towards sandstone cliffs. From the top of these cliffs visitors have excellent views of Hlotse and the Hlotse river. Follow the path, between the block houses, and take the right-hand path that climbs the slope to the summit.

The B25 road continues east through clusters of Lombardy poplar trees. Hlotse's suburbs creep east for about 4 km before abruptly ending below the Mahla Restaurant. Then, after a single steep hill, travellers will find themselves driving over a flat plateau before dropping to the Lesiamo Primary School and cultivated lands, with an interesting hardware store on the right: M. Hoosens. This store provides everything that locals could want: food, timber, paraffin and blankets. Although no longer part of Hlotse, the valleys are still heavily populated. This continues as far as the B1 Garage and Leseli City Restaurant. From the restaurant the road begins winding into low hills. Visitors with their own transport should be alert for stray animals; there are no fences and the herdboys are too busy practising stick-fighting to bother about their animals.

Concrete and tin houses are soon replaced by traditional stone and thatch huts. The valleys become less populated, filled instead with wild flowers during summer and ponds of ice in winter. At the Bafokeng General Café, a crowd of old people usually sits talking the day away. Some of them speak English and if you have time, they recount interesting stories from their youth and the dramatic changes they have seen in their valley.

Before the little town of **Pitseng** you will encounter the Pontmai Mission and Sikies Supermarket. The supermarket is not much more than a pub, but the school provides a preview of what visitors can expect from the people further east. The schoolchildren will stand for hours watching foreigners, with some occasionally trying their English, much to the amusement of their friends.

Fuel is available in Pitseng, but only at the bus and minibus taxi rank on the crest of the hill climbing into the town. (Don't be fooled by the Petrol and Gas sign pointing further out of town.) The London Restaurant behind the fuel station offers cheap and filling meals. The best tasting and most popular of these is the roasted chicken wings with papad brown bread.

Pitseng is a dirty, noisy town and unless going to the Outward Bound School, few travellers stop here. If you must sleep over, ask at the London Restaurant for the London Lodge. A few maloti will secure you a rusty bed-frame, cold water and a tin roof. If no programmes are being run at the Outward Bound School, visitors will find a bunk-bed or a tent pitch there. It is, however, out of town and unless you have your own transport, you may find it too far from the bus and minibus taxi rank in Pitseng. Most of the staff at the school are friendly and the instructors, who enjoy chatting to visitors, have travelled extensively. A fee is seldom asked, but travellers should leave a donation. This not only keeps the site open to future visitors, but helps in the running of the school.

Leaving Pitseng, the road dips through a cleft in the hills and passes a sign reading "Welcome to the Lesotho Highlands Water Scheme. Katse Dam 100 km". From here travellers leave the lowlands and begin climbing towards the mountains. The road dips to cross the Bolahla River, then rises past traditional villages. The B25 begins to make a series of sharp turns as it hugs the contours of the hills to make the gradient less steep. Ahead, visitors will see the road twisting its way up to the Mafika Lisiu Pass (3 090 m). Take note of the warning signs which caution of snow, ice and winds. Turn off to the view-point at the top of the pass and gaze down into the lowlands of western Lesotho. This area is frequently plagued by thick mist, rain and strong winds. Travellers on motorbikes or bicycles should be careful and alert; monstrous construction trucks carrying heavy machinery use this road, and in the mist and rain they find it difficult to see small vehicles or pedestrians. From the pass it is a long descent into the next valley. The mountains close in around the road and, apart from the river rushing past in the valley, there is nothing to disturb the silence.

LEJONE

Lejone is the next village, and although fuel is not available, there is a bed and meal to be found at the Malibamatso Lodge. The lodge, to the left of the B25 road, is clearly signposted. It falls into the medium tariff category, and has six rooms all with washing facilities. Seldom visited, Lejone does have a few things to offer visitors. Staff at the lodge can organise fishing in the surrounding rivers and a pony-trek into the mountains. Lejone is a traditional Basotho village, and even though there are European teachers at the school, foreigners are still regarded with interest.

Beyond Mamahau Mission and Mukateng Shopping Centre, the road is cut from the sheer sides of the mountain, with a vertical drop to the one side and a cliff climbing to the misty heights on the other. In the deep valley to the left, the LTA Construction Quarry ravages the once pristine valley floor and hillsides – all for the Lesotho Highlands Water Project.

This is a difficult road even in good weather, with hairpin bends and blind rises. It passes through villages which are a mixture of construction camps and traditional huts. Tin camps crowd along the road all the way to the bridge over the Matsoku river. Once the Highlands Water Project is complete, this bridge will be a mere 3 m above the water. An unusual method of construction was used in building the bridge: once the concrete pillars had been laid, sections were cast and then launched over the chasm. Only after the initial base had reached the other side was the road tarred.

There is a steep climb from the bridge, up to the Laitsoka Pass (2 650 m). Magnificent views can be seen from the summit of the pass, across deep valleys and wide rivers. High-voltage electricity cables overhead are a somewhat jarring sight.

South of the pass, travellers skirt Mahopela village before entering **Seshoto** settlement. This is undoubtedly a sheep-herding village, and the scent is strong. The Sekekete Store and Restaurant is bare, but the beer is cold and the meal on offer, mutton stew, is hot and tasty. Seshoto is the site of the local hammer-mill, and on weekdays there are queues of people waiting their turn to grind sorghum or maize. Little English is spoken, but the open faces and wide smiles are words enough. Across the shallow valley is a gravel airstrip, used mostly by the foreign construction planes. For visitors without transport, this is a good place to hitch a plane out of Lesotho or to one of the other remote construction sites.

Leaving Seshoto, the road climbs steeply to the top of Nkaobee Pass (2 510 m). There is even a lonely bus stop at the summit of the pass. Villages lie scattered around the valleys, but stone walls and thatch roofs make them difficult to see as they blend in with the slopes. There is something thought-provoking about the way tribal people always try to make everything in their lives round, from their houses to their cooking pots.

The tarred road changes in appearance from here, and what was earlier a grey surface is brightened by flecks of white in the laying compound. To the south of the pass there is a profusion of flowers during late summer. Past the flower fields, visitors enter a narrow gorge, which grudgingly allows the road at the bottom of the towering Water Project dams. There is a strong military and police presence, and you will be required to stop at two red-and-white checkpoints. Parking is not allowed and obviously taking photos will land visitors in custody at Katse village. A rise follows, to a T-junction, from which one track leads to Katse village and the other onto a gravel road, south to Thaba Tseka.

Katse village and Bokong are pretty much off limits to non-construction personnel, and it is an ugly place anyway – a conservationist's nightmare of prefabricated huts, iron roofs and the rumble of heavy machinery. There is a lodge at Katse village, but most travellers have found it almost impossible to get accommodation. Most of the rooms are pre-booked by construction crews and the security guard will not allow you to enter unless you can prove that you are employed by a company working on the Highlands Water Project.

Back at the T-junction, fuel is available from the Bokong Store. Visitors travelling to Thaba Tseka on public transport should get off here. Thaba Tseka lies about 65 km south along a good gravel road. About 12 km along this road is another security checkpoint, and then the road continues into the wilderness of central Lesotho. The guards at this checkpoint have a reputation for being difficult, but a few cigarettes usually seem to get travellers through the boom quickly. The locals get friendlier and keen to practise their English as you progress along the road. Most of the road passes along an undulating plateau, with the Malibamatso river flowing in the deep valley to the east, and the peaks surrounding Thaba Tseka to the south.

THABA TSEKA

A new town by Lesotho standards, Thaba Tseka was officially opened on 12 March 1980. The reason for its development was the need to have a capital for the mountainous area. Most of the funds for the development of the town came from a Canadian aid project. The Lesotho government in conjunction with the Canadians planned the town to be a model of how towns should be built in the remote areas of the country. Large agricultural schemes are in evidence, and attention is given to grassland management, water systems and soil conservation for the highland regions. Its high altitude makes Thaba Tseka cold most of the year. In summer there are frequent thunderstorms, while in winter snow on the hills and biting winds are common.

Orientation

Thaba Tseka is 174 km from Maseru. Entering the town from Katse, travellers drive up a slight rise, heavily populated on both sides. To the left is the Paray Hospital. The town sprawls across two hillsides in a north-south direction. Most of the original settlement is draped across the northern hill, while the newer suburbs are clustered together on the southern slope.

For visitors to Thaba Tseka, important sections of town are at the top of the rise into town, and to the south. The former is where the bus and minibus taxi stop is, and the traditional shops are located. Across the footbridge, at the southern side of Thaba Tseka, are the post office, bank, accommodation and RLMP (police) station.

Once you have taken note of the different slopes on which the town lies, it becomes simple to find your way around. Thaba Tseka is small and it is always possible to see both sides of the town, unless you are visiting the Paray Hospital. The older section of the town will be of interest to visitors keen on meeting locals, while the modern area will hold a fascination for those interested in Basotho ponies or ageing agricultural gear.

Information

There is one bank in Thaba Tseka, and it is in a trailer, near the block houses fitted with solar panels. Check on hours of business because the bank is sometimes closed at the strangest of times: 11h00 on Monday or 14h30 on Thursday afternoon. There has obviously been a lot of planning concerning the purpose of Thaba Tseka, but little in the way of town planning. Apart from a few modern houses in orderly rows, the business district grows in any direction. There are no roads between the buildings and footpaths have become thoroughfares.

The post office has no signboard and if it weren't for the post boxes outside, a visitor might never find it. Go to the bank and look towards the red-and-white radio mast. About 50 m away, below the mast, is the post office. Few of the staff speak English, but sign language seems to be sufficient. Being so isolated in the midst of towering mountains the telephone system in Thaba Tseka is problematic. Trying to make an international call requires a lot of time and patience. If there have been storms or strong winds, don't even bother. The postal service is however efficient. Medical attention is available at Paray Hospital; foreigners must pay, then claim from their insurance.

Numerous buses crowd the main road through old Thaba Tseka, above the Maluti Mountain Brewery. Transport arriving in and departing from Thaba Tseka congregates in the same place, but travellers must ask the street vendors who throng the area which bus is going where. There is one minibus taxi serving this remote region, and it travels from Katse village to Thaba Tseka only. Buses leave for Maseru at about 6h30, with the last one departing at 13h30. The minibus taxi to Katse leaves from the same place at around 09h00.

Hitching out of Thaba Tseka is difficult as most of the traffic is either government or aid vehicles, neither of which is likely to pick up foreigners. Occasionally a private vehicle will travel out of Thaba Tseka, and if you are determined to hitch there are two places to wait. To Maseru: wait at the T-junction where the road from Katse meets the road going west. This is on the northern side of town below the old BP filling station. For lifts going south or east: stand on the bend to the south of the Agricultural Training Centre or near the Basotho pony stud farm. Some lifts will be free, other drivers will expect a fee for yourself and your luggage.

Fuel is available at Thaba Tseka, about 2 km from town at Fraser's Store. Take the road to the T-junction which divides the northern and southern parts of Thaba Tseka. At the T-junction there is a signboard pointing the way to Mokhotlong, Thaba Tseka and Thaba Tseka Store. Take the gravel road going south-west to Thaba Tseka Store. The road passes through a small forest and ends in the middle of a village. Continue through the gap in the dry-stone wall and immediately turn right, up the potholed track. This track curves to the left after about 50 m and leads to the large silver-painted fuel tanks.

There is also an airstrip on the southern side of the town, still new but already trying to hide itself in long grass and even taller weeds. According to the Chief of Police, airplanes seldom use the town and travellers should rather try a method other than flying to get to and from Thaba Tseka.

Things to see

Even though Thaba Tseka is a new town, there are a number of interesting sights for visitors to see. There is something for everyone visiting the town. As in all Lesotho towns, the best way to see the sights is to leave your transport at the RLMP (police) or at the Agricultural Training Centre. Walking through the town is the best way of getting the larger picture of Thaba Tseka, as the paths and roads link both the old and the new. Visitors are just as likely to encounter blanketed women carrying bundles of wood on their heads, as they are to see new 4x4 aid vehicles.

Thaba Tseka Skills Training Centre

Situated on the modern side of Thaba Tseka, the Skills Training Centre is an interesting place to visit. Follow the gravel road towards the sewerage farm. This road passes the University of Lesotho Agricultural Buildings. The Skills Training Centre is located in a facebrick and tin-roof complex and falls under the jurisdiction of the Lesotho Ministry of Education. It has been set up with assistance from foreign aid packages and is part of the U.N. Development Programme. A yellow sign at the entrance to the offices notifies people that no visitors are allowed, but the office staff are friendly and will gladly turn a blind eye to the orders.

The purpose of the Skills Training Centre is to encourage the locals to acquire training in some facet that will improve their standard of living and income. The fact that training is based on what they already know enables them to reach what aid workers consider to be an economically viable standard of work. A number of courses are under way for most of the year and visitors will be able to watch skills being used that have been carried on in Lesotho since the birth of the nation.

Basotho pony stud farm

This magnificent farm lies to the south of town, and for visitors interested in horses it is a must. The breeding project is carried out with the assistance of Irish Government aid to Lesotho. Take the road that passes the RLMP station and Agricultural Training Centre and continue out of town, on the road to Mokhotlong. The stud is enclosed by a wooden fence and well-fertilised paddocks. Although the farm is not the Basotho Pony-riding Centre, the stud manager is willing to provide visitors with a few ponies and a guide for an hour's ride. Recently an Italian visitor was able to buy a pony from the stud, and see Lesotho on his own pony. The manager is friendly and takes visitors around the stables and grounds, explaining the workings of the stud, its aims and problems. Obviously a great deal of effort and financial aid have been put into the stud; the negative side to this is that visitors are not permitted to wander around, and must be accompanied by the manager or someone duly appointed to the task. But do not let this put you off walking around the grounds, which are more reminiscent of an English farm than of Africa. There are ponies in most of the paddocks – these are the brood mares and stallions which keep the blood of the Basotho pony progeny pure.

Around town

After seeing the above-mentioned sights, the next thing for visitors to do is spend a few hours drifting through the two sections of Thaba Tseka. There are European volunteer workers in the town, but the sight of a foreigner walking the streets is still something of a novelty to the locals, who will talk to you and invite you into their homes. One route to follow starts at the Agricultural Training Centre in the southern part of town. From here take the road that goes past the Skills Training Centre and University of Lesotho (supported by the Genesis Foundation). This road passes the affluent suburbs and ends at the plumbing store, which consists of a fenced yard full of PVC plumbing supplies that seem to have been forgotten amidst the wild flowers trying to reclaim the site for nature. Turn left at the yard and continue along the path towards the slope that goes down to the stream separating the two sections of Thaba Tseka. To the left of the path is another fenced yard, this one full of unused agricultural equipment bearing labels of the Canadian International Development Agency.

Interviewing the founder of the Lesotho News Agency made clear the dilemma of aid to Third World countries. Three types of aid package are made available to Lesotho: aid for development, upliftment and employment (this type of aid is rare); aid for a given project (such as the Basotho pony project); and aid with strings attached (the most common and, according to the Basotho, the least helpful type). Ask any number of Basothos about aid programmes and the common complaint is that the locals are not consulted before the project is implemented. This leads to suppressed anger towards the people responsible for the project.

From the house on the left, marked by a ground-level solar panel, the path branches into several paths, all converging on the green footbridge over the stream. Pedestrians, for whom the bridge was meant, must be prepared to share space on it with sheep, goats and often cattle. This results in some exciting moments, especially early in the morning, as shepherds try to get their flocks across to the southern bank and smartly dressed, attaché-carrying businessmen attempt to reach the bus stop. The bridge also appears to be the meeting place of the town's schoolchildren who vie with one another to throw the most rubbish into the stream. Lesotho is a country of contradictions and paradoxes; most travellers leaving the country return home with a different perspective on many things.

Once you have crossed the bridge, there is a climb up the terraced slope to the bus stop. The women in the stone houses to the right of the path are considered the best brewers of traditional beer in Thaba Tseka. At the top of the hill, the old town is a bustling and colourful place. There are several small shops, including a hair salon, photo-developing kiosk, shoestore, sewing shop and cafés. Further east are larger stores, such as the Basia Café, beyond which lie the northern suburbs of Thaba Tseka scattered across the hillside. Visitors can get to the Paray Hospital by threading their way between vegetable gardens and livestock yards in these suburbs. The hospital is always busy, and although the medical staff tend to be harassed and overworked, visitors are free to wander through the grounds and outdoor wards.

Past the hospital is a deep gorge around which shepherds graze their flocks. Exploring this gorge can yield some interesting finds including fossils, shards of clay pottery, tin cans and what look like the remnants of cave paintings.

A gravel road turning off from the A3 national road, which passes the bus stop, is only about 80 m long and provides access to the "mixed" area of Thaba Tseka. Go past Fraser's Cash and Carry and the Maluti Mountain Brewery entrance. This is only a depot for the brewery, but visitors can look inside the sheds after asking the General Manager's permission. About 20 m further is the Sunshine Café, and across from that is a shopping complex. Behind the Sunshine Café are large market gardens. Travellers can visit the gardens, and the foreman will walk around the site with you, explaining each vegetable that is cultivated. This model market garden could become one of the stops on Lesotho's proposed Environment-Tour package.

At the shopping complex across from the Sunshine Café, visitors will be able to see a traditional Basotho butchery at work (not recommended for those with weak stomachs), a bakery, knitting and sewing shop and cafés selling everything from beer to shoes. From the shopping complex a path leads east and crosses the stream in the valley.

Back on the lower slopes of southern Thaba Tseka you will find the district government offices, whose staff work to their own hours. Behind these buildings is a cattle and sheep shed, and behind that, on the edge of a cliff, a Youth Centre. There are usually people at the centre and it is the gathering site for the town's teenagers. They play netball, soccer and loud music, but whatever the noise levels, it is a peaceful and happy place. It is possible to get back to your starting point by taking the path that winds between the sewerage ponds and small dams and joins the road going to the Agricultural Training Centre.

Places to stay

Thaba Tseka has no tourist accommodation, although an overnight facility has been proposed and will be built within 10 years. Few visitors spend time in Thaba Tseka as it seems to have little to offer. This is a pity, as it is a good example, in microcosm, of a country in transition: politically, socially and culturally.

Agricultural Training Centre (low tariff)

The centre is in the southern suburbs of Thaba Tseka, along the road that turns right behind the RLMP (police). There is no sign indicating the centre, but travellers will find the long prefabricated buildings 20 m beyond a stone and thatch rondavel. During the week the centre is full of people, but over weekends it is often empty. Visitors hoping to stay at the centre can go to the Agricultural Office, or to house number B10 across the road, where the matron of the centre lives.

There is accommodation in 12 rooms, a variety of empty offices and occasionally even a caravan. The official rooms are furnished with sliding drawers, wooden double-decker bunk-beds, foam mattresses and, if requested, clean bedding. There is no canteen or restaurant, but kitchen facilities are available. There are showers and toilets in the official accommodation area, and this is the time when a pair of plastic shower sandals would prove valuable. A walk up the hill behind the centre offers a panoramic view of Thaba Tseka, as well as the chance to see some of the agricultural training lands and animals of the Agricultural Training Centre. The centre is also a good place to meet Basothos involved in the training, either as students or as lecturers. Few people make reservations before arriving in Thaba Tseka, but those who would prefer to do so should write to:

Address: The Accommodations Registrar, Agricultural Training Centre, P.O. Box 125, Thaba Tseka, Lesotho
Telephone: (09266) 900304

Camping (free)

This is the easiest way of staying in Thaba Tseka. The town is not spread out, and a short walk in any direction will have you in a wilderness area of villages or isolated trading stores. The most attractive place to pitch a tent is in the little forest below the Water Department office. Ask permission from the Officer Commanding Thaba Tseka RLMP; he is helpful and jovial and is likely to take you to the forest himself, indicating points that might be of interest and even advising on where to eat. A stream flows through this forest and there are a number of level sites for a comfortable pitch. Cold water is available at the stables, and should it rain, there is always an empty box with a thick bedding of fresh straw.

Another spectacular setting is behind the Youth Centre. The land overlooks a river, cliffs and mountains which form a natural boundary to the south-east of Thaba Tseka. Get permission at either the government offices or from the caretaker of the Youth Centre who is usually willing to provide a bucket of hot water for washing. If you asked at the Youth Centre, it is good policy to leave a donation. These youth centres play an integral part in the developing Basotho Youth Programme, and each donation is ploughed back into the running of the centres. Apart from these sites, campers will find many places to set up a tent, and as crime is almost non-existent in Thaba Tseka, campers will be safe.

Other possibilities

If you are desperate for accommodation, approach the teachers at the Paray School. They are always glad to meet foreigners and will try to find you a bed for the night. For adventurous visitors: go into any of the pubs, order a beer and sit back to wait. Within an hour you will have made several new friends and will probably be offered a bed and meal in one of their homes. This is obviously the mercenary way of doing things, and visitors accepting this hospitality should contribute to the meal or offer some payment for the bed.

Places to eat

Just as Thaba Tseka is limited on proper tourist accommodation, there is a dearth of restaurants in the form of what visitors might be used to. There are no à la carte menus or lavish dinners to be had. But there are many Basotho-style restaurants, mainly in the older part of Thaba Tseka. Eating at these establishments is one of the great experiences of Lesotho, and until you have tried dining at a Basotho restaurant, you have not fully encountered the Basotho. There are no fixed meal times, and visitors will notice diners coming in off the street at all times of the day and late into the night, some to eat, others to drink, and a few just to sit and look at the others or stare at the foreigner.

In the shopping complex across from the Sunshine Café are a number of shops selling food. For meat eaters with strong constitutions, mutton or lamb can be bought at the butchery. Next to the butchery is a bakery that makes delicious "makwenya," fried dough cakes. Behind the bakery is a courtyard of odd shops. The café sells fresh bread, milk and a few tinned goods. At the bus stop there are many street vendors who sell fruit, vegetables and mutton stew or chicken curry accompanied by papad bread. Further west, good meals can be had at either of the two large stores on the right of the road, near Khotsong General Dealer.

For vegetarians, a good place to try is the market gardens behind the Maluti Mountain Brewery. The foreman will let you pick out vegetables, he will wash them (be careful: the water may be impure) and then mentally weigh the vegetables before charging you. Try the Basia Café on the road to the hospital, which has a wide selection of fresh fruit and vegetables on display. Fruit and vegetables can also be bought from Mothusi Fruit and Vegetable Café next to the Lesotho Bank. The only cheap meals in Thaba Tseka are those that are made locally, such as porridge, roasted or grilled mutton or lamb and local bread. Other foods, which must be transported over the mountain roads, are expensive.

Things to buy

Not being on the tourist trail, Thaba Tseka has little in the way of traditional Basotho handicrafts for sale. There are a few places however where items can be bought.

The Thaba Tseka Skills Training Centre occasionally has goods on sale, but this depends on the craft course being run at the time. Across from the Phokeng Store is Mohlalese's Knitting Centre. Both Basotho and imported wool can be purchased at the shop, and there are locally knitted jerseys and shawls at reasonable prices. A visit to one of the nearby villages could also prove worthwhile for those interested in buying traditional handicrafts. At Fraser's Store (the filling station), villagers will sometimes approach a visitor with something to sell. Avoid buying anything that looks antique or that might have something to do with tribal culture. Selling these artefacts has become a serious problem in many developing countries and is stripping their cultural heritage from the tribes.

Continuing west towards Maseru, travellers leave Thaba Tseka along the same road on which they entered. Go past the old BP filling station and Roads Department camp to the T-junction, where the road from Katse meets that from Maseru. It is signposted. Continue along this road, following the signs to Maseru. For about 4 km the road passes through villages surrounded by trees and small streams, then into a wide valley. From the plain, the road climbs in twists and bends up to the summit ridge of the mountains. Early in the morning the summit road is usually covered with ice or frost and travellers on motorbikes or bicycles should be careful. There is an incredible silence on this high road, and a feeling of euphoria, induced by the altitude and sense of freedom, is experienced by many visitors on this lonely mountain road. One traveller from Israel, who had already traversed the African continent, commented, "This is a place where people can grow, where the mind can search beyond its limited horizons."

About 11 km from Thaba Tseka the road drops to a wide alluvial plain. The area to the left, alongside the river, is a favourite camping spot for overlanders. Ask the chief at the village across the river for permission to camp on his land.

Beyond this plain the road once again climbs to the summit ridge in tight hairpin bends, which can be difficult to negotiate in the wet season with an overloaded bus. Rising through a narrow gorge in the hills, the road exits onto a plateau. The area is very isolated and largely uninhabited, except for the occasional shepherd and his flock. Further along the plateau the road rises to the Pass of the Jackals (2 700 m). Visitors should be on the lookout for the herd of wild horses that inhabits this area. Sometimes, if the herd is grazing near the road, the stallion can be seen standing sentry on the mountain to the left of the Pass of the Jackals sign.

From the pass the road descends through a valley before crossing the Mantsonyane river, then passes the Roads Department camp and forks into **Mantsonyane** or on towards Maseru. Fuel is available in the village, and it is a stop on the bus route from Maseru and Thaba Tseka.

To get into Mantsonyane, take the left fork in the road, at the signboard. Follow the single road through the middle of town to where it ends at a large red shed. To the right are the fuel tanks, some street stalls and numerous traders who patiently wait for the buses that arrive. To the left is an open area behind a dry-stone wall and Basotho trading stores. For the hungry traveller who enjoys eating traditional food, a visit to the Mantsonyane street sellers is a must. Their cooked meals are always hot, and they have a way of grilling chicken pieces over an open flame and serving them with brown bread that is delicious.

Continuing west, take the right fork in the road and go past the neatly tended garden on the right. Beyond the garden the road commences to climb. On Tuesdays the river behind the house is busy with washing activity, and although the women are suspicious of men watching them, they are delighted to have a foreign woman chatting to them while they work.

Leaving the valley, the gravel road rises through ever widening valleys until it reaches the summit of the Loqkhane Pass (2 560 m), where there is a weather research station. The sharper corners on the steep descent from the summit are partly tarred. This often proves a challenge to drivers who meet another vehicle coming up the hill: both want to stay on the tarred sections –the buses especially. It is much safer to pull over to the right of the road, alongside the vertical cliffs, and allow the other vehicle to pass.

Some small villages are passed on the way into the valley of the Senqunyane river. The Marakabei Lodge sits beyond a one-vehicle-wide bridge amidst groves of plane and poplar trees and heaps of building bricks. When no reservations have been made and the lodge is empty, visitors may find it closed and the staff unhelpful. The setting of the lodge is beautiful, and travellers wishing to spend time in this secluded valley should make reservations:

Address: The Manager, Fraser Lodge System, P.O. Box 5, Maseru, 100, Lesotho
Telephone: (09266) 322601

MARAKABEI

Past the Marakabei Lodge, the road skirts the edge of a steep hill overlooking a weir on the river, crests the hill and then drops to Marakabei village, about 47 km from Thaba Tseka. For visitors arriving by bus from either Maseru or Thaba Tseka: the bus does not go into Marakabei but stops on the A3 national road about 100 m from the village. To take a bus out of the village you will have to walk to the national road and flag down a passing bus.

Fuel is available in Marakabei, from Fraser's Store. To get to the store from the main road, go to the signpost for the primary school and follow the potholed gravel road to the left. This road crosses a stream and then passes through a stone wall before ending in an open area outside Fraser's Store.

Fraser's Store is worth a visit. Built of yellow sandstone blocks, it is the centre of business for the area and is always full of people dressed in traditional clothing. The area outside the store is also the site for street vendors. Their "makwenya" dough cakes are delicious, as is their lamb stew. Near the horse railing, old men sit and drink beer for hours in the sun, and are delighted to talk to a visitor for a while.

Marakabei is sheltered in a deep valley and although the nights can be cold, the days are warm.

Outside Marakabei the road begins to climb, with views getting more dramatic. There is a slight descent into Likalaneng, which boasts a shop that makes bright coffins, ranging in colour from pink to lime green, blue and red. One of the carpenters says that the Basotho prefer being buried in colourful coffins because the hole they are placed into is so dark.

Outside Likalaneng the gravel road climbs until, about 70 km from Thaba Tseka, travellers cross the windy crest of the Blue Mountain Pass (2 634 m). There is a radio relay station further up the mountain and an armed military sentry can usually be seen patrolling the perimeter fence. (Definitely no photographs are allowed.)

Approximately 2 km further west is the Basotho Pony-trekking Centre. Tucked into a fold of the heather-covered hills, the Pony Centre is situated at 2 318 m, and during winter is often covered in snow. Of interest to many visitors travelling this route through central Lesotho are the Triple Race and Endurance Race which take place from the Basotho Pony-trekking Centre from 6–8 May each year. Most of the competitors are farmers, who arrive from all over Lesotho with their ponies. Large crowds gather and buses arrive, carrying people from as far away as Mokhotlong and Moyeni (Quthing).

Another 2 km further is the Molimo Nthuse Lodge, part of the Lesotho Hotels chain. This lodge is built in a natural hollow alongside a fast flowing stream, and is sheltered by willow, plane, poplar and wattle trees. The lodge falls into the high tariff category, with the tariff covering bed only. There are 16 rooms, all with private bathroom, in a two-storey building. Upper-floor rooms all have fireplaces while ground-floor rooms have heaters, both of which are used even during summer. An à la carte menu is available. There is a selection of dishes, which are expensive and tend to be overcooked. English and Continental breakfasts are also offered. Both dining room and bar are in an enormous raised rondavel, with splendid views down into the Makhaleng river valley. The manager is able to arrange guides for day-hikes, trout fishing in the stream and, through the lodge's sister hotel in Maseru (Hotel Victoria), for transport to and from the Basotho Pony-trekking Centre for riding. November–January and April are the busiest months for the lodge, but outside these peak periods visitors will usually find accommodation. Make reservations with the Lesotho Hotels main office:

Address: The Reservations Manager, P.O. Box 212, Maseru, 100, Lesotho
Telephone: (09266) 322002/3

West of Molimo Nthuse Lodge the tarred road begins the climb to Bushman's Pass (2 226 m). The descent from the pass allows travellers wonderful views over cultivated fields and tin-roofed villages. In the valley to the south-west the old bridle path from the mountains to the lowlands can be seen making its dangerous route down.

At the bottom of the tarred road is the Tollgate Caravan and Camping Park, owned by Lesotho Hotels. Not many tourists visit this park and some buses travelling from Maseru refuse to stop here. There are concrete pads for 12 caravans and campers may pitch tents anywhere within the park. Small and near the busy A3 national road, the park is shielded by a hedge and has full ablution facilities. The Tollgate Bar is a good place for a cold beer but gets crowded over weekends. Reservations are never necessary and the manager seldom asks campers for payment. Cheap meals can be bought from several of the Basotho restaurants on either side of the national road. Snacks are available at the Tollgate Bar.

In the lowlands there is a noticeable change in the attitude of the people. The hospitality of the mountain clans is replaced by an indifference to foreigners. Hikers, bikers and cyclists should be careful of the children who seem to delight in throwing whatever is at hand as you pass. About 3 km west is the settlement of **Nazareth.** Visitors seldom stop here other than for fuel, or as the start of a walk to Ha Barona and the impressive gallery of Bushman paintings. Fuel is not always available at Nazareth, and the attendants will not inform you that their supplies are finished. If not served within five minutes, you can accept that no fuel is available. Make sure by asking at the snack shop.

You may leave your vehicle or the bus at the filling station in order to walk to the paintings. Take the path to the north of the garage, follow this for about 1 km and then turn left onto the track at the cluster of wattle trees, which shade a Friesland dairy. Continue along this track until it enters the village of **Matela** about 2 km away. This is an interesting walk that few visitors try – most drive to Matela from Maseru. At Matela you will be surrounded by a horde of children offering you their guide services to the paintings. Accepting is a good way of putting money directly into the locale. Visitors should choose a likely looking candidate; they all know their way around the galleries. Once again, as with other services in Lesotho, negotiate the price before you set off. The Bushman paintings are about another 4 km from Matela, with a shallow river crossing in between. (The Rural Services and Footbridge Development Board is soon to erect a wood and metal footbridge over the river.)

From Nazareth it is 14 km to the T-junction of the tarred road; either right to Maseru or left to Roma, about 8 km to the south-east.

ROMA

Given to the Roman Catholic Church in 1863 by King Moshoeshoe, Roma is the site of the first Roman Catholic Mission established in Lesotho. It was called Motse Oa Ma Jesus (village of the Mother of Jesus) by the first Catholic priests, Bishop Allard and Father Gerard (who has since been canonised by Pope John Paul II).

Roma is also the educational and spiritual heart of the sprawling Roma valley. The main campus of the National University of Lesotho is in Roma, as are a number of seminaries and a teachers' training college. Roma is full of students, both educational and spiritual, and many visitors find this town a peaceful and tranquil stop on the road to Semonkong about 85 km south-east.

Orientation

Lying in a north-south plan along the base of sandstone cliffs, Roma is surrounded by numerous varieties of trees. Visitors approaching from Maseru along the A5 national road will pass through the suburbs of town before reaching the business district around the University (N.U.L.).

Visitors will find most services, and a few of the sights too, clustered around the university main entrance along the national road. The north of town is relatively flat and spills into the beautiful Roma valley, while the southern side crouches below towering cliffs. Even side roads are tarred in Roma, which is surprising for a town that is not a district capital. Visitors will find their way around Roma easily if they navigate by the Observatory, on the hill across from the university. The Observatory can be seen from most points around town and provides a central reference while you explore the surrounding area. If you get lost, the many students who wander about Roma are always willing to give accurate, if rather verbose, directions.

Information

The university has "cash card" facilities for Lesotho banks. Across from the University entrance is a shopping complex that houses the Lesotho Bank, at which traveller's cheques can be cashed and money drawn on credit cards. Hours of business are Monday to Friday 09h00–13h00. In the same complex is a billiard hall, supermarket and some empty shops. Fuel can be obtained from the Roma Filling Station near the university, on the A5 national road.

The RLMP (police) are on the right of the road south, and this is a good place to leave your vehicle if you plan to spend only a few hours in Roma. The RLMP will park your vehicle behind the police station and assign a policeman to keep guard until your return. Across from the RLMP is the post office, next to the hedge which secludes the St Augustine Seminary. This post office is efficient and the staff are helpful and friendly. International calls can be booked through Maseru from the Roma post office, and if lines are not busy, visitors can expect an immediate connection. The Postmaster is prepared to keep letters mailed to poste restante, but with the post office at Maseru only 35 km away travellers seldom bother.

Buses and minibus taxis regularly travel the route from Roma to Maseru, and congregate in two different places. Buses stop near the post office and about 200 m north of the university. Minibus taxis line up outside the Roman Catholic Mission, about 1 km south of the post office, in the afternoon, and near the Shell Filling Station in the morning. There are scheduled times of arrival and departure for buses, but travellers can expect the bus to arrive or depart about 15 to 30 minutes either side of that time. This does not prove an inconvenience as there are many buses travelling between Roma and Maseru. For buses south to Semonkong, passengers should be at the bus stop at least an hour before the bus is due to leave. There is only one daily bus to Semonkong, which leaves around 8h30. Minibus taxis leave when full, and visitors will have to ask drivers their destinations. Although minibus taxis travel south of Roma, few go as far as Semonkong, and travellers going there may have to make a series of minibus taxi "hops".

Things to see

Roma and the surrounding area have something to interest most people, from historical buildings and educational centres to hikes around the magnificent valley and Bushman paintings in the eastern cliffs. Sights are best experienced by leaving your transport and walking.

Roman Catholic Mission

The mission is about 1 km south of the post office. Established in 1862, the mission charts the development of Roma. It offers visitors a glance into Basotho history, into a time when the Basotho nation was still young and foreigners brought Christianity to Lesotho.

Enter the mission through the dry-stone wall, where the statue of Mother Mary blesses Catholics, schoolchildren and visitors alike. Take the track to the right, which squeezes past the church and ends at the ecclesiastical offices. Before you walk around the grounds ask the Father in Charge for his permission, and if he is unavailable ask one of the junior Fathers who can usually be found in the office.

Begin a tour of the mission by visiting the Bishop's sandstone house and private chapel behind the main office. These are both built around a small courtyard and date from the early days of the mission. Turn right at the office, go past the garages and empty fuel bowsers, and continue along the path which borders a fruit orchard to the left and rises above the church to the right. There are numerous sandstone buildings along the right of the path. One cannot help but get the impression that although the mission must have been well managed and impressive many years ago, it is now somewhat neglected. Most of the old buildings near the church are used as storehouses, halls and sometimes classrooms for the school.

Following the path north towards town, visitors will pass through a gate in a dry-stone wall, below a dark dam, and then walk along a path lined with conifers and eucalypts. Early morning and evening the trees give off a heady scent which adds to the celestial atmosphere of the surroundings. Among the widely spaced trees to the east of the path are the remains of a dairy, piggery and other livestock buildings. They are no longer used, and the barn has become a secluded place for teenage couples. Beyond the barn is a house below the cliff, rented out; the arable lands below are cultivated. For good sunset views, follow the path that leads up next to the huge boulder, on the south side of the colourful rented house. This path winds its way, through forest and bush, to a slope that rises to the summit plateau of the sandstone cliffs. The summit affords views to the western hills.

Back at the centre of the mission, no matter what your faith, visit the church and soak in the silence before stepping out into the real Lesotho again. As at other missions in Lesotho, a donation for the opportunity of seeing the mission is always welcome and goes a long way towards the enormous costs of keeping missions operating in Third-World countries.

University

Located in the central business district of Roma, the university offers visitors an opportunity to see one of the top educational centres in Africa. Started in 1945 by the Roman Catholic Church, and once part of the South African Catholic University College, the university is now under the jurisdiction of the Ministry of Education. With an enrolment of over 1 000, the university attracts students from many parts of the African continent, including Botswana, Zaïre, Tanzania and Nigeria.

Enter the university from the A5 national road; you may be asked to sign in at the security desk. Visitors are allowed to walk around the campus and through the maze of buildings spread across the grounds. There is not a great deal of historical interest at the university, but it is a serene place with a studious silence, disturbed only over weekends when the students abandon their books for boisterous parties and sports events.

Touring the entire campus can be tiring. Visitors should rather go to the reception office in the brick building, at the end of the drive from the entrance, and ask for directions to particular faculties or the library, which is well stocked and provides visitors with a wealth of information about Lesotho. Most of the university campus is shaded by trees and carpeted with well maintained lawns, and visitors are welcome to have a picnic beneath the trees.

Most students are friendly, and even though there are foreign lecturers at the university, they are always interested in visitors. You can expect to be approached by students as you walk about; some want to say "Hello," others want to know more about your home country. Should you be interested in a particular subject, the women at reception are helpful and will direct you to a lecturer knowledgeable on that subject. Reports from other visitors seem to confirm a trend that is common in Lesotho: non-Basothos are not friendly or helpful towards travellers, while locals are. Do not be surprised at a number of oddities at the university, for example: the Dean of the Faculty of Agriculture is from Nigeria, a country that is hot and dry in the north, with scorching Sirocco desert winds, and hot and wet – humid most of the year – in the south. One can hardly imagine a country more unlike the cold, wet and mountainous Lesotho.

When leaving the campus you are required to sign out at the security gate.

Observatory ruins

Next to the Lesotho Bank, across from the university, is a round stone building which houses a hair salon and photo-development kiosk. Follow the gravel path that leads between the hair salon and the café. The path becomes a tree-lined avenue which leads to the ruins on the hill. The entrance to the remains of the Observatory is through two stone pillars and then either right or left through breaks in the fence. Although visitors have to share the grounds with cows, sheep, goats and curious children, there are excellent views of Roma and the valley.

The site is no longer cared for, which is a pity since it could be turned into a tourist attraction. There does not seem to be any exact answer as to the origins and history of the Observatory, and visitors will be told different versions depending on whom they ask. The grave of a Roman Catholic Father can be seen next to the two entrance pillars. This grave has led to the suggestion that the Observatory was built by this Father, who died before the structure was completed. Whatever the truth concerning the construction of the buildings, the one accepted fact is that the Observatory was aligned with certain trees and mountains in the valley to provide astronomical reference points for observations.

Clambering around on the structures is interesting and offers visitors a tour of blind passages, uncompleted staircases, empty towers and Latin inscriptions. Students often sit studying in various parts of the Observatory and lose themselves in their books and the silence.

Places to stay

Roma does not have any tourist accommodation, and trying to find lodging is difficult. Most students live on campus and those who do not are either from the area or stay in "digs" in the suburbs. For visitors not concerned about luxury and comfort, camping anywhere in the Roma valley is a pleasant experience, and allows you to hike in the hills and valleys that encircle the town.

Roman Catholic Mission (free)

The mission is about 1 km south of the university. The Father in Charge is willing to allow visitors to sleep at the mission and will provide a room, washing facilities and even meals. For singles and doubles, accommodation is in a private room with bathroom, toilet and shower. The Sisters also supply guests with soap, towels and fresh bed linen. During winter, a gas-fired heater warms up even the coldest of nights. Accommodation is clean and airy with a simplicity and serenity that makes up for any lack of luxury.

Camping is also possible on the mission grounds and a particularly attractive pitch is in the fruit orchard next to the Bishop's sandstone house. Campers may wash in any of the empty rooms and the Sisters will bring buckets of hot water for cooking and dishwashing.

The mission is an ideal place from which to explore Roma and the valley. The Father in Charge has spent many years in the area and can offer visitors a wealth of history and information about Roma. When you leave the mission, give a suitable donation for the accommodation. Although the accommodation is seldom used, it is still considerate to book in advance, though travellers who just turn up are never turned away.

Address: Roma Roman Catholic Mission, P.O. Box 11, Roma, Lesotho
Telephone: (09266) 340204

Camping (free)

Camping is what most visitors who intend exploring the Roma area choose. There are interesting and spectacular pitches in the many hills and shallow valleys that make up the area. Always ask permission where you wish to camp, and try to camp well away from any water, otherwise you will be bothered by numerous flying insects. Campers should try to camp near the RLMP (police) or the mission, or well away from town. When camping in the Roma valley, you will attract curious villagers who provide an opportunity for meeting the locals and, sometimes, even of finding an unofficial guide to the hills.

Places to eat

Finding a decent meal in Roma is difficult. Most of the population are students who either eat at their institutional canteens or carry light meals from their lodgings. The eating houses available are, as everything else seems to be, near the university campus. A few cafés and restaurants can be found down the sidestreet across from the Roma Mission. It is a good idea for visitors to Roma to bring their own food.

Those who are staying at the mission may eat meals there, but if you are desperately hungry, a sandwich will be made for you. Meals at the mission are simple but filling, and visitors wishing to eat with the Fathers and Sisters should ask in advance, so that extra places can be laid.

Food can be bought from the large supermarket in the shopping complex across from the university. Tinned meat, fresh vegetables and snacks are on sale. The problem with buying food at the supermarket is that foreigners are quickly surrounded by children who shout, "Give me sweets! Give me money!" This begging must not be encouraged.

North of the hair salon, at the entrance to the Observatory, is a gravel path that leads to a brightly coloured eating and drinking house, which offers one dish only: porridge with mutton. The meal is cheap and, though greasy, filling and tasty. The cook will wrap the meal in brown paper if you would rather have a take-away. Friday and Saturday evenings the restaurant is busy and travellers can spend a few interesting hours talking to the locals who patronise the place.

Near this restaurant is a small corrugated-iron dairy on the right along the path to the Observatory, about 100 m from the national road. The cows are milked at 07h00 and again at 16h30. Visitors who have their own bottles can buy 1 or 2 litres of fresh milk from the dairyman who milks the cows.

Eggs can be bought at the Roma Egg Circle near the shopping complex. Find out, before buying them, how long the eggs have been there. (A number of Basotho die every year from Salmonella poisoning.)

Things to buy

Roma has no curios for visitors, but with the close proximity of Maseru and the many tourist shops available there, few visitors bother looking for things to buy in Roma. The Book Centre, near the university, has books on sale that might be of interest to visitors, but the university library is better stocked, as are the magazine and book shops in Maseru.

Travelling south from Roma, visitors pass the Roma Mission and School and then through a suburb with tidy gardens bordered with trees. A few shops and cafés also line the road. About 3 km south of the mission, along the tarred road which has begun to climb through a gap in the sandstone cliffs, a gravel road branches to the right. This narrow road, which becomes a track, edges a cliff and then cuts up to the summit on which stands a cross as a blessing on the Roma valley below.

The A5 national road continues south to Thaba Chita primary school at the summit of the Ngakana Pass (2 035 m), over the crest of a hill and on towards the Thaba-Putsoa mountain range. The Thabana-Li-Mele Women and Youth Training Centre, 18 km from Roma, is situated in a grove of trees on the left of the southbound A5. Here visitors can buy superb handmade arts and crafts. Weekdays are best for viewing the range of traditional items on sale. There is no bargaining system at the training centre and the asked price is what visitors are expected to pay. The quality of wares on sale is high and compares favourably with that of any curio store in Maseru.

For travellers heading further south towards Semonkong, the road passes across two causeways before reaching a T-junction 20 km from Roma, in the village of Moitsupeli. To the right the B45 road swings north towards Maseru, and crosses Motseki's Pass (1 995 m). To the left the A5 remains tarred for 150 m before becoming gravel. Three kilometres out of Moitsupeli, travellers will see the twin peaks of Thabana-Li-Mele (for which the Women and Youth Training Centre is named), which means "breasts of a woman".

Visitors with their own transport should be alert for livestock on the road. Wednesday morning is stock sale time in the villages around Roma, and stockmen bring their animals in along the road from the higher settlements.

About 8 km further, visitors climb the Nkesi Pass (2 020 m) before dropping into a deep valley and the village of **Ramabanta** on the Makhaleng river. There is not much to see in Ramabanta and fuel is not available. What might be of interest to Land-Rover owners is that this appears to be the Land-Rover spares capital of Lesotho. Numerous Land-Rovers stand alongside the main road, all in various stages of being either stripped or rebuilt.

Beyond Ramabanta the gravel road rises through hillsides covered in wild flowers and sheep flocks. On the steep sections the road is tarred. Higher up the thick vegetation gives way to sparse moorland

and clumps of grey heather. This road from Ramabanta into the mountains will be a nightmare for riders of motorbikes and bicycles: the road is covered by small sharp pebbles that make traction difficult, and any shift in your luggage could cause you to fall.

The maize and sorghum fields give way to wheat and oats the further south you travel into the mountains. Even the character of the people changes; they become reserved and simpler in their lifestyle. Most of the isolated villages consist of round stone huts with thatch roofs and walled-in animal enclosures. Finally there is a long descent to the wide and sluggishly flowing Maletsunyane river, and a fork in the road; either over the weir and on to Semonkong, or right to Lebihan Falls. Visitors usually go into Semonkong, and from there decide how they will visit the falls.

SEMONKONG

Semonkong means "Place of Smoke," and is so named because of the Lebihan Falls. Father Francois Le Bihan was the first European to see the falls, in 1881, and they are named after him. Semonkong has an untamed feeling, and is still far off the main routes around Lesotho. Once the secret hideout of smugglers and outlaws it remains a centre for the remote villages in the surrounding mountains.

Orientation

Lying in a west-east direction, Semonkong is 113 km from Maseru and 78 km from Roma. Entering town, travellers will find directions from the weir crossing by following the large red Fraser's Lodge signboard. The road passes the St Leonard Roman Catholic Mission on the right and becomes the main thoroughfare through Semonkong.

Services for visitors can be found around the bus stop at the left turn into the business area of town. This is where the bank, post office, most shops and restaurants are located. The road through Semonkong is in an atrocious condition and drivers are expected to find their own safe route across the dongas, mud and rocks. Getting one's bearings around Semonkong is not difficult: all points in town and in the surrounding countryside are accessible from the main road.

Information

There is no official Tourist Information Centre in Semonkong, but the staff at the Mountain Delight Lodge, at the eastern end of the main road, and Fraser's Lodge, near the Forestry Department Nursery, are helpful and friendly.

The post office and Lesotho Agricultural Bank are close together in the busiest part of town, near the corner at the western approach to the main road. Although officially an agricultural bank, the bank is prepared to cash traveller's cheques but cannot accept credit cards or hard currency in exchange for Maloti. The postal workers are somewhat offhanded with foreigners, and it goes without saying that this remote town has no poste restante service. Telephone services are erratic and dependent on the weather for connections to the rest of Lesotho.

Buses congregate in the open area across from the bank. There is one bus between Maseru and Semonkong each day. The trip takes about seven hours if the roads are in good condition. The bus leaves Semonkong early and tends to fill up quickly, and travellers should jump on at the bus fuel depot about 50 m behind the bank, on the road entering town.

Fuel is available at Fraser's Store. This is the large red building across from the airport, at the eastern end of the main road. Note that the store only opens at 8h30; fuel is obtainable about 15 minutes after that. Follow the road to the airport control tower and then turn into the open gateway leading to Fraser's Store.

Things to see

Semonkong has several sights that will interest visitors. Most require a fair amount of walking but provide an opportunity for getting to meet the locals, many of whom are descendants of smugglers and outlaws. Many visitors prefer to drive between sites and this is advisable for those not accustomed to strenuous walking. For those who are, the best method of seeing Semonkong and what it has to offer is to leave your transport at one of the lodges, take a small day-pack and set off exploring.

Lebihan Falls

This is undoubtedly the major tourist attraction of Semonkong. About 5 km south of Semonkong, the falls are a must for visitors. They are among the highest on the African continent, and the highest single-drop falls, at 192 m, in southern Africa. Lebihan Falls are best seen during the wet summer months, when the increased volume of water makes them a magnificent sight. The falls were once accessible only on foot or by pony, but a good gravel road has now been built and visitors can drive to the view-points.

To drive to the falls, go back to the river crossing at the fork in the A5 national road, and then turn left. This junction is marked by the

Fraser's Lodge sign. Continue along this road, through sandstone villages, down onto a small plateau. The road makes a sharp turn to the left along the crest of a hill, and then drops to the view-point above and across from the falls. Be careful on the windy spur over the gorge, especially young children and elderly people.

Other alternatives to reaching the falls are either on foot or by pony. Ponies can be arranged at both Fraser's Lodge and Mountain Delight Lodge. Hiring ponies and a guide can be expensive and many visitors opt for the time-consuming, but more comfortable and cheaper, hike to the falls. Both walkers and ponies follow the same route, which begins behind Thatcher's Tavern at Fraser's Lodge. Follow the rocky track up behind the lodge and go through the broken fence onto a cultivated hillside. Take the left path over the crest, and down into the terraced valley. Continue along the track, over the little stream and up through a village. Take the left path, which curves up past a house with an exquisitely carved front door and then reaches the top of the hill near another Fraser's Store. Several paths come together at this point, and visitors should aim for the large tin shearing shed to the south-east. Go past the shed and continue alongside the security-fenced area to the left. The path then dips into a shallow valley with stunted conifers to the left and cliffs to the right. At the wide gravel road, turn left and follow the road to the ledge overlooking the falls. To get to the bottom of the falls requires the services of a guide, which can be arranged at Fraser's Lodge. The walk to the top of the falls takes about one to two hours there and about one and a half hours back, while the trip to the bottom of the gorge three to four hours there and at least five hours back. Both places offer spectacular views of the falls and their accompanying rainbows, which play against the dark shadows in the eroded cliffs.

The setting of the Lebihan Falls is awesome, with plummeting cliffs, strong updraughts and an eerie atmosphere. When the larger towns of Lesotho get overwhelming, this is the place to which visitors should escape.

To get back to Semonkong, walkers who have a head for heights should try another route. Instead of returning up the hill along the road, take the path that skirts the large crack to the left of the view-point. This path follows the cliffs around the gorge and provides magnificent views into the pools and gulleys that surround the waterfall. At the curve in the path behind the strangely shaped rock formation in the gulley, turn left and up the hill. This will bring you out near the tin shearing shed you had passed on your way to the falls. From here, retrace your route to Fraser's Lodge and then on to Semonkong.

Around Semonkong

Pleasant hours can be spent exploring Semonkong and its environs. Start a walk from Fraser's Store near the airport, but instead of following the main road through town, take the path that runs parallel to the main road between the dry-stone walls. There is a broken gate just past the livestock holding pens at the store, through which walkers should pass. Continue along this path, which passes the soccer field on the right and a number of traditional stone houses on the left. The track then skirts a brightly painted pink house among burial mounds. This is rather an odd place for a cemetery, but according to the Officer in Charge at the RLMP station behind Fraser's Store, the Basotho people, although supposedly Christians, still believe strongly in the animist faith and prefer having their cemeteries in populated areas.

Walk alongside the cemetery, and visit the hair salon on the left, in the little courtyard of stone houses. Imagine having a Parisian hairstyle done here! A few metres further the track joins a road that dips between cultivated vegetable and cereal plots, to the Forestry Division's Nursery on a bend in the river. There is always activity at the nursery and visitors are free to wander around looking at the trees that are being grown. Most of the employees are women, but there is a foreman who speaks good English and is enthusiastic about his job, especially when it comes to telling visitors about the work that is carried out at this isolated little nursery deep in the mountains. The road ends at Fraser's Lodge and becomes a track to the hill villages and Lebihan Falls.

Turn back towards town at the pink house; the road goes past modern block houses to the open-air blockmaking factory behind the Sunshine General Café. Beyond the café is the business area of Semonkong. Next to the Lesotho Agricultural Bank is a carpentry workshop which makes basic furniture, grim coffins and a few turned statues. Across from the carpentry workshop, near the bus stop, is a statue of a Basotho shepherd. Created in 1987 by a German sculptor, the statue is a tribute to the resolute and tenacious Basotho who inhabit this remote and challenging area of Lesotho.

There are numerous hiking opportunities around Semonkong. Visitors who intend travelling into the mountains should be adequately prepared for sudden changes in weather. An interesting day-hike commences at the airport and follows the road to the left of the Mountain Delight Lodge. Then take the first gravel road to the right and loop back across the river near the RLMP (police). Follow the track along the side of the hills until it reaches the summit ridge above town. Turn left on the summit and go down into the valley of the Maletsunyane river to where it tumbles over the Lebihan Falls about 3 km away. This circuitous hike takes between four and five hours to complete; it is strenuous but passes through spectacular countryside, which makes the effort worthwhile.

Places to stay

Visitors to Semonkong will find three types of accommodation available: fully catered lodge, self-catering lodge and camping. The price difference is noticeable, especially between the fully catered and self-catering lodges. But there is accommodation to suit most pockets and visitors will have no trouble finding a place to sleep.

Mountain Delight Lodge (high tariff)

This quaint little lodge is at the eastern end of the main road through Semonkong, and although some distance from the Lebihan Falls, is a good place from which to explore the town and surrounding hills. It is about 150 m from the airport, an advantage to those visitors arriving by air and without any transport to carry their luggage. Tending to be noisy because of its location, the lodge does provide secluded accommodation within a closed area, off the main road. The capable manager is fluent in English and although not from Semonkong, has a good knowledge of the district. Few of the staff speak any language other than Sesotho, and visitors will have to do most of their communicating via the manager. Both ponies and guides can be arranged at the lodge, and guests should specify whether they intend visiting only the falls or also some of the remote mountain villages.

The lodge has 10 stone and thatch rondavels available to guests, all with private bathroom. Water and electricity are frequently cut off, and many visitors find themselves missing out on a wash and going to sleep by the soft light of candles. The rondavels are kept scrupulously clean and the manager's attention to detail has made the accommodation at the Mountain Delight Lodge of the best in Lesotho. The high tariff covers room and tea only; a dining room and private bar are open to residents. Unlike other lodges in the country, this one does not have an à la carte menu, and visitors are compelled to eat whatever the expensive set menu is for that particular day. (This will cause problems for visitors who are vegetarians.) A small but well-stocked tuckshop has a few basic foodstuffs and commodities. Reservations are recommended during summer and autumn, as this is when most visitors come to see the falls. Winter and spring are quiet at the lodge and travellers are certain to find accommodation.

Address: Mountain Delight Lodge, P.O. Box 7423, Maseru, 100, Lesotho, or The Manager, P.O. Box 8, Semonkong, 120, Lesotho
Telephone: (09266) 325577 or 311157

Fraser's Semonkong Lodge (medium tariff)

Fraser's Lodge nestles 1 km out of Semonkong in a deep valley on the edge of a rushing mountain stream. When you enter Semonkong, instead of turning left along the main street towards the airport, continue south past the Sunshine General Café. At the T-junction, about 80 m further, turn right past the little cemetery and follow the signs to Fraser's Semonkong Lodge. This road is graded regularly, which makes it fine for four-wheel drive vehicles, but difficult for two-wheelers. Continue down the road, round the bend at the Forestry Nursery, and across the stone bridge to where the road ends at the entrance to Fraser's Lodge.

The manager is friendly and has a great deal of information on local and more southerly areas of Lesotho. He is able to organise ponies and guides, and will assist travellers who want to pony-trek or hike from Semonkong to Malealea, about three days away to the west. Accommodation is self-catering, and is provided in 10 rooms which are either stone and thatch or wood and thatch bungalows; five have private bathroom and toilet. The remaining five bungalows share a central washing and toilet block, which is also available to campers who pitch on the lodge grounds. An equipped communal kitchen and dining room complete the facilities. A restaurant is being built on the site of the present Thatcher's Tavern. The tavern is cosy and quiet, and apart from a few locals who occasionally use the bar, visitors will be alone while they sip their drinks and watch the hypnotic flow of the stream. Reservations are recommended throughout the year, as this is a lodge to which people who have stayed once will return again and again.

Address: The Reservations Manager, Fraser Lodge System, P.O. Box 5, Maseru, 100, Lesotho, or Fraser Lodge Reservations, P.O. Box 243, Ficksburg 0730, South Africa
Telephone: (09266) 322601, or South Africa (05192) 2730

Camping (low tariff or free)

Excellent sites and facilities are available to campers who choose to camp in the grounds of Fraser's Semonkong Lodge. A charge is levied only if the washing and cooking facilities are used. This is a beautiful and tranquil place to set a tent and is a good spot from which to visit the Lebihan Falls, about two hours' walk to the south.

Camping is also available at the St Leonard Roman Catholic Mission about 1 km outside Semonkong, on the A5 national road linking Semonkong to Roma and Maseru. The Fathers at the mission are amiable and always happy to meet visitors. If room is available, campers will be invited to sleep in the mission instead. Washing facilities are provided, and simple tasty meals can be arranged. This is a wonderful experience, as you will be invited to eat with the members of the mission, something that few travellers ever experience. Should you make use of the mission, remember to give a suitable contribution when you leave. Many budget travellers make use of the mission and it is close to the starting point for the 2–4 day hike south-east across the mountains to Christ the King or Nkau. During summer and autumn the mission is a good place for meeting other travellers and exchanging information on different parts of Lesotho.

It is inadvisable to camp in the open anywhere too near town: reports of theft and harassment have been received from a few visitors. Rather go into one of the side valleys running off the main Maletsunyane valley and get permission from the chief at one of the villages tucked into folds of the hills.

Places to eat

A remote town, Semonkong has a limited range of eating places, and those available are either expensive or have nothing for the vegetarian visitor. Most food is imported, which tends to raise the price when compared to similar food in Roma or Maseru. It is better to take your own food supplies when you visit Semonkong.

Bland and expensive meals can be eaten in the dining room of the Mountain Delight Lodge. The set meals are enormous and difficult to finish, even after a day's walking. There is an English breakfast, while lunch and dinner are usually soup, meat or fish with boiled vegetables and either fried chips or mashed potato. Lunch and dinner end with tinned fruit and tea or coffee. Non-residents of the lodge must book for meals, especially in the tourist season, in summer and autumn. A fast-food service is also available from 08h30–16h30. There is a fairly extensive menu to choose from, and the variety of food runs from roasted chicken heads and feet, through Russians (sausages) and chips, to "makwenya" dough cakes and cold drinks.

Basotho restaurants are always interesting, and no journey to Semonkong is complete without a visit to one. The Woodpecker Restaurant and Fast Foods, on the corner across from the bank, is a busy and cheerful place. It is full throughout the day and a seat may be difficult to find. Those people who cannot find place often sit on the steps outside where they seem to enjoy their meals as much as inside. The restaurant is more a pub than a place to eat, but meals can be ordered. Don't expect a written menu, the assistant will simply tell you – usually in Sesotho –what is available and you decide. Mutton stews and curries are delicious, but the porridge can be a bit crusty. Cutlery is not used, and the best way to eat is to order some papad bread with which to scoop up the sauce. It can be rather a strange sensation sitting in the Woodpecker Restaurant and listening to pop music, while outside men on ponies canter past into the setting sun.

Food can also be found in any number of unmarked eating establishments at the western end of Semonkong. Just wander through the streets: an indication that food might be available is a fluttering white flag or plastic packet indicating that Basotho beer is on sale. Most of these restaurants and cafés on the fringes of town are a stimulant to the imagination. Renowned for its wild and outlaw past, Semonkong seems to attract mysterious characters. Visit any of the dark cafés and watch the men who sit behind bottles of beer whispering to one another secretively from under blankets. As the night moves on and candles are lit, the atmosphere of intrigue and danger gets thicker.

Compared to other towns in Lesotho, there are few street vendors in Semonkong. Apart from the wares of a few fruit and vegetable sellers, there is not much in the way of food for sale on the streets. Visitors planning to camp or stay at Fraser's Semonkong Lodge should bring food from Maseru and buy only the necessities in Semonkong.

Things to buy

There are no tourist curio or craft shops in Semonkong, but at the carpentry workshop near the Lesotho Agricultural Bank visitors can sometimes find wooden statues for sale. These are not always on display and buyers should approach the men working inside the barn-like structure. Price is highly negotiable and the haggling can take a considerable length of time, which can be shortened by inviting the sculptor for a drink at the Woodpecker Restaurant.

Another good purchase for visitors to Semonkong is a Basotho blanket. Semonkong is a mountain town; the icy winds howl down into the valley for most of the day, and a blanket is the best way of keeping warm. Fraser's Store, across from the airport, has a selection ranging from thin grey blankets to those with tassels and a colourful velvet finish.

The barmaid in the public bar at the Mountain Delight Lodge can arrange to take visitors to some of the surrounding villages where naturally dyed handmade blankets and carpets can be bought.

Semonkong is still very much a wilderness town, and if you are prepared to spend a few hours with the locals, an interpreter will soon be found to translate the often hideous legends of the area. And, as you walk home under a star-filled sky, it becomes clear that, sadly, this is one the last outlaw towns left in the world. Semonkong is more than just the Lebihan Falls; it is a journey into the world of horsemen, mountain storms and raging waters: a place that has never really left the pages of history.

For travellers who had decided earlier to turn right towards Maseru instead of left to Roma, the good tarred road continues west until reaching a fuel filling station about 3 km further on. Maseru is about 18 km further west. To the right, the road is signposted as going to Thaba Bosiu.

THABA BOSIU

Thaba Bosiu is the site of King Moshoeshoe's second and most important mountain stronghold. Buses to Thaba Bosiu can be caught in Maseru, but if you are arriving from the mountain road, get off at the Thaba Bosiu turnoff and stand along the B20 road where you can flag down a minibus taxi or bus which will take you to the fortress site. The Mmelesi Lodge is near the fortress, but foreigners seldom stay there, preferring the similarly priced but higher standard accommodation in nearby Maseru.

With the many flat-topped hills in the area it may appear impossible to find the right mountain, but about 100 m north of the lodge is a Tourist Information Centre, directly across from the main pass to the Thaba Bosiu mountain fortress. It is compulsory for visitors to hire a guide from the Tourist Information Centre. There is a small fee for the service. Usually one to three guides are available to take parties up the mountain. Try to get Mr E.M. Moshoeshoe, the senior warden, to guide you. He is a descendant of Moshoeshoe's 132nd wife and is not only well informed, but very passionate about the history of the Basotho and, in particular, Thaba Bosiu.

There are seven passes onto the summit plateau, but most visitors take either the "route of the brave," which is steep and slippery and leads up between boulders, or the "route of the cowards," which, although longer, is more gentle.

Moshoeshoe the Great arrived at Thaba Bosiu on 23 June 1824, having trekked with his people for nine days from Butha Buthe. Tragedy befell him on the route as his 90-year-old grandfather and 11 children were captured and eaten by cannibals. Chief Name', who ruled the region at the time, allowed Moshoeshoe to occupy this flat-topped mountain, which spies sent out earlier had chosen as a suitable place. The mountain has 11 water springs, plenty of grazing and trees. On their arrival at the mountain Moshoeshoe and his warriors spent from 21h00–05h00 building a stone wall across the steep entrance pass to the summit. The remains of this wall can still be seen by visitors who choose the "route of the brave" up the mountain. The name Thaba Bosiu means "mountain of night" because the Basotho had arrived in the evening and then spent the night strengthening the mountain's defence.

Although Moshoeshoe stayed on the summit plateau until his death at sunrise on Friday, 11 March 1870, his stay was fraught with problems. In 1827 the Mathewane tribe attacked the fortress but was defeated, and in 1829 Chief Sekonhela of the Baktlokwa tribe tried to dislodge the Basotho and was also repulsed. The Griquas tried in 1830 and were defeated, as was the Matabele chief, Mzilikazi, in 1831. From 1851 it was the turn of the British who unsuccessfully tried to overthrow Moshoeshoe: Major Warden from Bloemfontein in 1851, George Cathcart in 1852, Colonel Senekal in 1858. Then the Boers tried from 1865–68. Moshoeshoe remained invincible on top of his mountain.

In 1865 President J.H. Brand sent Boer forces marching on Thaba Bosiu. It was the largest military operation seen by the Basotho: 2 125 troops under 10 commanders. The lure for the Boer troops was the promise of land from the conquered Basotho. But the attack on the mountain fortress was a disaster from the start: Commandant Wepener, one of the senior Boer leaders, was killed in the first attack, along with 42 soldiers. Wepener was first stoned and then shot from the top of the "route of the brave". The site where he fell is marked. Unable to retrieve the body of their commander, the Boers were forced to wait until darkness before sending out a party. This dubious honour fell to Christian Durant and Carl Matthee. Under threat of attack they carried Wepener's body further up the mountain, past the protective wall, and buried him in a shallow grave to the left of the path.

Once on the summit, visitors will be explained the layout of the mountain fortress. They will be invited to place a symbolic round stone on the pile near the entrance to the Royal enclosure and recite a prayer to the Great King Moshoeshoe, founder of the Basotho nation. Remains of the original houses can be seen, including the square stone house where the King died, as can the burial tomb of King Moshoeshoe and other early Basothos. The tour takes two to three hours and is an adventure into the history of Lesotho. From the spot where one of Moshoeshoe's sons threw himself to his death because he had been forbidden to marry the girl he loved, visitors will be able to see the strangely shaped peak named Qiloane by the original residents of Lesotho, the Bushmen.

The summit of the mountain fortress is usually covered in wild flowers which bend to the gentle breeze that constantly blows across the plateau. The views in all directions are impressive, and it does not take a military genius to see why this mountain was chosen. This is one tourist attraction that should not be missed on a visit to Lesotho; it is the essence of the origins of the country and its people. Without experiencing the spirit that blankets the summit of Thaba Bosiu, visitors will have missed out on a basic understanding of the Basotho.

When you leave Thaba Bosiu to go south, pass the Mmelesi Lodge and take the first tarred road to the right. Continue through Mosalla village and take the right fork in the road, across the river, up the steep hill, back onto the tarred road and past the irrigation schemes. The sprinklers are not calibrated and spray as much water on the road as on the fields: bikers and cyclists should be careful of the slippery surface. About 50 m past the irrigated fields is a T-junction. Take the left turn, marked as **Maseru**. This tarred road winds through settlements until reaching the congested and polluted suburbs of south-eastern Maseru. Stay on this road as far as the T-junction with the Main South 1 road. Turn right onto the Main South 1, travel past the new bus and minibus taxi depot and to the circle at Our Lady of Victories Cathedral. The road to the left of the circle, Kingsway, will take you into the business district of Maseru. The exit opposite the Main South 1, Moshoeshoe Road, goes to the industrial and market area of Maseru. Three-quarters of the way round the circle, Main North 1 takes you north of Maseru and along the western lowlands of Lesotho. (This described route continues along the Main North 1 towards Teyateyaneng.)

Maseru's north-eastern suburbs sprawl in a tangle of gravel roads, modern houses and shanties. Traffic is heavy along this section of the route, and visitors travelling the A1 national road over weekends should beware of drunken drivers and large construction vehicles.

There is a gap in houses before Ha Foso village, the land being intensively cultivated. Beyond Ha Foso the road is an avenue lined with English poplars, which in the autumn are a splash of reds, oranges and browns. The terrain changes to flat-topped sandstone hills and narrow valleys. There is a slight rise in the road past numerous handicraft centres and then into Teyateyaneng.

TEYATEYANENG

Meaning the "place of shifting sand" Teyateyaneng, or TY as it is commonly called, is named after the quicksand in the river about 500 m out of town. Founded in 1886 as an administrative centre for the British occupation forces, the town still has relics from that time. Capital of the Berea district, TY is also the site of many handicraft centres. It has the reputation of being the friendliest town in Lesotho.

Orientation

TY is 42 km north-east of Maseru on the A1 tarred road. It is draped over a hill in a south-north plan, with a single main road, the national road, running through the eastern side of town.

Of relevance to visitors are the areas alongside the A1 and around the Blue Mountain Inn in the western part of TY. The post office, hotel, banks, shops, handicraft centres and business area are located to the west of the A1, while along the A1 are restaurants, fuel stations and public transport depots. The southern area of TY houses the mission, Basotho cafés and concrete houses. To the north and east, TY rolls away into suburbia – obviously a wealthy town: most of the houses are made of brick and cement.

Orientation in TY can be difficult because of the way the town lies over a hill. Possibly the best place to use for finding your bearings is the Khotso Restaurant, across from the old disused church, on the crest of the hill over which TY is spread. About 100 m north, along the A1, are a number of gravel roads going east into the residential area of TY. Further north is the large Y-junction of the road to the business district. Wherever you end up while wandering about town, the best landmark to ask for if you are lost is the Blue Mountain Inn. Most locals seem to know where it is, and once you have asked at least three people you may safely follow the route given. Visitors who ask at a dwelling for directions are often invited in for a beer or a meal before someone is despatched to guide you to your destination.

Information

The post office, Blue Mountain Inn and a few cafés are along the road that branches west from the A1 national road to the north of the disused church. Most of the shops are on the left side of the road, while the post office (marked as "ost ofce"), cafés and the inn are on the right. It is possible to make international calls from the post office in TY, but the service is slow and unreliable so visitors should rather book a call through the inn, about 200 m west along the same road. A same-day dry cleaning service is available at JR Dry Cleaners, which lies midway along the first road that runs to the right, west of the old church: go past the Off-sales Bottle Store as far as MS Supermarket; the dry cleaner is across the road.

Standard Chartered Bank is across from Ellerines Furnishers, near JR Dry Cleaners. Barclays Bank is next to Supreme Furnishers in the same road as the Blue Mountain Inn.

Numerous buses and minibus taxis serve TY. For those travelling to the northern regions of Lesotho, public transport gathers outside the three-storey Bright Star Wholesalers' building at the northern end of the town, near the Y-junction. Transport to the south leaves from outside the Khotso Restaurant, on the top of the hill on which TY lies. For hitchhikers, the best place to wait for lifts going north is about 50 m beyond the three-story building along the A1; if you want to go south, walk out of town and wait near the entrance to St Agnes Mission and Handicraft Centre. Hitchhikers and travellers using minibus taxis should enquire and fix a price before setting off.

Fuel can usually be bought from the Caltex Fairdeal Motors and Filling Station on the A1. If there is no fuel supply at Caltex, you can buy a few litres, at a higher price, from the minibus taxi drivers outside the Khotso Restaurant.

About 20 m north of the Y-junction, across from C.M. Motor Spares, is the sign pointing the way to the Maluti Hospital. With Maseru only 42 km away and the South African town of Ficksburg 43 km to the north, visitors who need medical treatment seldom stop here.

Things to see

Teyateyaneng does not have many sites of historical or cultural interest, but for visitors who enjoy shopping without the rush, few towns can rival it (see Things to buy). TY is one of the few towns in the country where visitors can reach most sites of interest by road, other than having to scramble around the sandstone cliffs to look for Bushman paintings. Still, many visitors prefer to park their vehicle at the inn and wander through the town as the mood takes them.

TY's sights are essentially clustered within a 3 km radius of the post office, and travellers gain more by walking among the people and houses than by driving. In this way visitors get to experience TY's famed hospitality: you will seldom walk more than 100 m without being approached by a local, just for a chat, or sometimes to be invited into their homes. (I was invited to a local headman's wedding – a unique experience.)

Bushmen paintings

There are Bushmen paintings in a number of the surrounding sandstone hills. Go south-east out of town for about 2 km, along the gravel B203 road. There is a path going south, just to the right of the traditional beer seller's stone and thatch house. Follow this path to the Teja Tejane river. Turn either up or downstream and begin exploring the many shallow caves and overhangs in the sandstone cliffs. If you decide to turn upriver, you can expect to be joined by herdboys who will help you find some of the paintings, many of which have been damaged by tourists and locals who sell the sheets of stone. But for visitors who do not mind a little danger, to the south of TY there are still clear and surprisingly descriptive paintings, in the caves 10–20 m above the two rivers that flow near each other in the valley.

Around town

For many visitors a walk around TY is a wonderful way of seeing life in a district town. An interesting walk can be taken by following a circular route back to your starting place. Begin at the post office, across from the TY Four Square Centre. Go past the café that pumps loud reggae music from broken speakers, then turn left at the Blue Mountain Inn Off-sales and down the road past the bank, until you reach an opening on the left which houses a traditional mud and thatch hut. On Saturday evenings this hut is the meeting place for local elders. Dressed in blankets and hats they sit for hours, eating roast mutton and porridge, and consuming vast quantities of canned and locally brewed beer. Visitors who pass by can expect a friendly greeting and an invitation to join the gathering. You may not understand all that is said, but every once in a while someone will translate some point of particular importance.

Continue along the road to the Y-junction and turn right (south) at the Capital Fast Foods café. The TY Hall is on the left, 10 m up the road, and behind it is the Lioli Football Stadium. Football matches are played on Sundays, and visitors should make an effort to attend one of these games. The normally soft-spoken Basotho supporters lose all inhibitions when the players enter the field. With loud shouting, singing and dancing they rally their teams. Unlike European and South American fans, these spectators seldom cause any unpleasantness, and apart from a few drunks falling over, there is no tension or violence.

South of the TY Hall are public toilets on the left, and on the right is the archetypical "crooked house". Every feature of this house appears to have been purposely built unbalanced: drooping window sills, a sagging door, an angled thatch roof and a bumpy earthen courtyard with crooked chairs.

Across from the Caltex Filling Station, visitors will find Phalima livestock yard. Read the blackboard outside, which displays Today's Specials: Sheep, Goat, Cow.

Across from the road-route marker for Maseru, Teyateyaneng and Sefikong is a pedestrian alley to the west. On one Friday evening per month, a local "battle of the bands" is held in the small grassy area behind the first tin-roofed house. The music is very African, and though it is played distortingly loud on old speakers, this is an ideal place to meet both young and old residents of TY.

Continuing south, past the road-route marker, walkers will come to the T-junction where they should turn right, past the sandstone church and street vendors. At Fairways and Brown's Cash and Carry, turn left down the hedged road. This way leads to the more affluent suburbs of TY. Travellers will find the local children friendly; they often follow foreigners, laughing and talking to you. Turn right at the first gravel road and walk along a lane to an open area in the vicinity of Setsoto Design Workshop. Follow the road north up the hill. It soon becomes obvious that most of the non-Basotho people living in TY hide themselves behind high fences and walls, many of which can be seen on this section of the walk. The Basotho women who live in the compound behind the wooden fence, on the left of this road, may offer to do your washing. Their fee is minimal, and if the washing is delivered before 09h00, it can be collected clean and ironed the same day.

At the top of the road, where it joins the tarred road, you will see the entrance to the Blue Mountain Inn on the opposite corner, and a few residential houses before you end at the post office again.

Places to stay

TY has limited accommodation. There is only one hotel and camping is feasible only a few kilometres beyond the suburbs. TY is within striking distance of larger towns within Lesotho and in South Africa, and travellers who intend staying here will find accommodation expensive. If you are prepared to mix with the locals, however, you are likely to be offered a bed for the night. Not many visitors try this option but the opportunity to live with a Basotho family, even if only for a night, should not be missed.

Blue Mountain Inn (high tariff)

This small hotel is situated on the right of the road, about 1 km west of the A1. There are signs pointing the way to the blue and white painted hotel. Set among tall evergreen trees in a peaceful garden, the Blue Mountain Inn is an unexpected luxury. The hotel is clean and boasts committed and helpful staff. Pony-trekking can be arranged through the manager, as can guides to the handicraft centres.

There are 16 rooms, all with private bathroom, in bungalow-style accommodation; visitors are also provided with television and heating units. The rooms are spacious, with fitted cupboards, wall-to-wall carpeting and clean bedding on the double beds. Room tariff includes morning tea but excludes all meals, which means that visitors may choose to eat in the comfortable dining room. Breakfast is especially pleasant; the dining room's large windows afford a clear view of the gracious garden and fenced swimming pool. Menus are à la carte and offer a good, if somewhat expensive, variety of food. For those with their own transport, 24-hour security and covered parking are provided. There are also two public bars and a snooker room.

The main attraction at the inn is however the Blue Night Club/Disco. On Saturday evenings this is really the place to be. Doors open at 21h00 and close around 06h00. It's pointless trying to sleep through the steady beat of African and Western music, so many visitors choose to join in the fun at the disco. The disco gets very crowded from about midnight, and to find a seat you should try to get there, at the latest, by 22h30. Alcohol is on sale, as is a certain noxious weed. Be careful if you do decide to partake: cannabis is illegal in Lesotho and the occasional RLMP (police) raids always result in a few arrests and imprisonments. Music shifts from traditional African rhythms to the latest European sounds and there is bound to be something that you can dance to. Foreigners will be regarded with curiosity for a while, but then someone (of either sex) will approach and ask if you would like to dance. You'll then be invited to meet his or her friends and within minutes the ice between you will have been broken.

Reservations are not necessary, but can be made if you wish. Note that, as in other district hotels, the management of the inn is reluctant to accept credit cards.

Address: The Manager, Blue Mountain Inn, P.O. Box 7, Teyateyaneng, Lesotho
Telephone: (09266) 500362

Places to eat

Having the busiest road in the country, the A1, running through it, TY has many eating and drinking spots, catering mostly for meat eaters and alcohol drinkers. Other visitors can buy fresh fruit and vegetables from the many street vendors who set up their stalls around the empty church, at the sign pointing the way into Teyateyaneng. Haggling over the price of food from these vendors hardly seems worth the effort when you discover the pittance they ask. They do seem to take offence, though, if you just go right ahead and pay their first asking price.

Meals are also available in the dining room of the Blue Mountain Inn. There is an à la carte menu for lunch and dinner, and meals are substantial and well prepared. Service is slow as many of the dishes are only prepared once the order has been placed. This has the advantage of giving visitors the chance to relax and have a drink in the cosy residents' bar before being called to eat. The menu has a full complement of starters, main courses and sweets, including options for vegetarians. A small but select wine menu is also available.

Visitors will soon notice the proliferation of restaurants and fast-food shops in TY. About 60 m west of the A1 national road, in the same road as the inn, the Monate Café offers fresh fish and chips served with salt and vinegar in newspaper. Capital Fast Foods, at the Y-junction near the northern end of town, has a large menu of fried foods. On the slope of the hill leading to the southern part of TY is the Holy Cross Café and Fast Foods, offering items ranging from sheep's heads to Russians (sausages) and chips. This café is a health inspector's nightmare and visitors should avoid anything but hot, freshly fried food from it. On the crest of the hill is the Khotso Restaurant which has basic meals aimed at the Basotho palate, and is the favourite haunt of minibus taxi drivers. (If necessary, use the opportunity of eating here to arrange transport out of TY.) The chicken curry, eaten with "makwenya" dough cakes and washed down with a bottle of cold beer, is tasty and filling. West towards the post office, the Casaloma Store has a few basic commodities, such as stale cookies, warm fizzy drinks, beer and tinned food.

Things to buy

Teyateyaneng has long been a town that attracts visitors who come to shop. There are weaving factories, a knitting centre and other interesting handicraft workshops. All offer visitors a vast array of goods both traditional and modern. For travellers who want to buy some mementoes of Lesotho, TY is a lot cheaper than Maseru and has just as many crafts from which to choose.

When entering from the south, visitors will pass the sign to St Agnes Mission and Helang Basali Handicrafts on the right of the A1 national road. The missionaries at this centre have taken Basotho creativity and channelled it into the weaving of colourful rugs and descriptive tapestries. Prices are reasonable and, apart from some of the funds going back into the running of the centre and mission, money goes to the workers themselves. This is one of the weaving centres at which the whole production process can be witnessed. The centre is open to customers and visitors 08h00–17h00 every day of the week.

Across the road from the Blue Mountain Inn is a gravel road going to Letlutlo Handicrafts, which has a selection of traditional products, all handmade, mainly in pure wool.

Near the TY Four Square Centre at the sign reading "Best Men Smoke Best Blend", is the sign for the Setsoto Handweaving Centre. Open 08h00–17h00 on weekdays and 08h00–12h00 on Saturdays, this design and production centre is a model home industry. It has a large foreign clientele, and prices are high, but the amount of work that goes into the magnificent handwoven tapestries, colourful cushion covers, placemats and raw wool jerseys more than justifies the expense.

Travelling north from Teyateyaneng, on the A1 national road, visitors drop into a valley to cross the Berea district boundary on the bridge over the Phuthiatsana river. About 10 km from TY is the much publicised Kolonyama Pottery Kiln and Beadazzled Jewellery. Beneath a large flat-topped hill with sandstone cliffs, this little village is synonymous with intricately designed and well crafted pottery products. Visitors are welcome to tour the facilities, watching as the potters turn mounds of clay into collector's items. There is a bewildering array of pottery from which to choose, ranging from painted dinner sets to cups and animal statues. This has become an obligatory stop on the tourist trail, and prices at Kolonyama Pottery have soared during recent years. The matter will have to be reconsidered if the costs are not to drive customers away to other, less expensive, potters.

Near Kolonyama Pottery, in the same open courtyard, is Beadazzled Jewellery. Here beads, wood and soft metal are crafted by hand into tasteful necklaces, ethnic earrings and colourful bracelets. An indication of the price range is that all major credit cards are accepted.

Another 33 km north is the border post with South Africa, where the central route ends at the bustling town of Maputsoe.

SOUTHERN ROUTE

From MASERU – MORIJA – MAFETENG – MOHALE'S HOEK – MOYENI (QUTHING) – QACHA'S NEK – SEHLABATHEBE NATIONAL PARK
Distance: about 470 km
Road indicators: A2, A4, A15, B33

From MASERU

To commence the southern route take the Main North 1 from Cathedral Circle in Maseru towards Teyateyaneng. About 3 km from the circle are traffic lights, near the Lakeside Hotel. This road is signposted for Mafeteng and Moshoeshoe International Airport. For travellers using public transport: take a bus or minibus taxi from Pitso Ground bus terminal. Hitchhikers should get to the Lakeside Hotel, and then hitch from the pull-off area to the left of the hotel entrance.

On this road visitors pass through the cluttered suburbs of southern Maseru. There are filling stations on this road, but it is not necessary that you fill up here, as fuel is available at frequent intervals along the southern route. The turnoff to Moshoeshoe International Airport is 20 km from Maseru. This is a busy road and hitchhikers will have no problem in finding a ride. Continue along the A2 national road. A little beyond the airport is a sign giving the distances to Morija and Mafeteng.

About 3 km beyond the airport, on the right, is a large flat-topped mountain which dominates the valley, and which is worth a walk. Travel through Mantsebo village and leave your transport at Qeme Holdings. The manager is friendly and will take care of your vehicle until you return; on weekends the security guard prefers drivers to park their vehicles outside his hut rather than in the grounds of Qeme Holdings. Walk along the track to the south of the factory, between block houses, to the river. Cross the river and continue on the track which becomes a path some 100 m further. The path edges an impressive donga, in which several soil profiles can be seen. Once you are on the slope above the donga, follow the path to the right, which climbs a spur onto the mountain summit. Walk north along the summit for about 50 m, and then onto the sandstone ledge that overhangs the cliffs. There is a spectacular view across the valley, over Moshoeshoe Airport, agricultural fields and the distant settlement of Mazenod.

From Qeme Holdings the road goes through **Masite** village, where fuel is available. After Masite there is a change in the topography. Hills begin to crowd the valleys, and although low, they are steep, with sections of cliffs. Getting deeper into a range of hills, the road twists over slopes before dropping to the historical town of Morija.

MORIJA

Nestled below towering sandstone cliffs, 45 km from Maseru, the Evangelical Spiritual Centre of Morija has several interesting sights for visitors, which include the Lesotho National Museum archives, dinosaur footprints and historical buildings dating from the early 1800s. Founded by French Protestant missionaries in 1833, Morija is named after Mount Moriah in Israel. With the oldest Christian church in Lesotho, Morija remains a centre for spiritual study and education.

There is no tourist accommodation, and unless you are willing to camp in the hills or stay at the Mophato Ecumenical Youth Centre, either return to Maseru or go south to Mafeteng. Sleeping accommodation is available at the Mophato Youth Centre, but it is basic and very cold during winter. Reservations, which are seldom necessary, can be made.

Address: The Warden/Youth Organiser, P.O. Box 6, Morija, 190, Lesotho
Telephone: (09266) 360219

Remember that on Sunday the museum and archives are closed, but you are welcome to attend a service in the sandstone church, built in 1834.

There is no organised tourist route and visitors should leave their transport outside the museum and wander around town. Visitors may also visit the high school started by the French, and look in on the Scott Hospital near the entrance to Morija. The curator at the museum and archives is knowledgeable about Basotho history; both the legends and the reality. And, as the dinosaur footprints are difficult to find, he will take visitors to the site. The footprints are in good condition and should be visited. Faint Bushmen paintings can also be seen by following the track that passes the high school above the museum. Walk for about 2 km into the small valley, and ask one of the herdboys to take you to the paintings – they are somewhat disappointing and have been vandalised (not really worth the strenuous walk).

If you go along the road east of Morija for 7 km, you will arrive at the Royal Settlement of **Matsieng**. This historical village is the birthplace of King Moshoeshoe II. There is not a great deal to see at Matsieng, but the village could be included in a circuit from Morija by travellers returning to Maseru.

As you leave Morija on the A2 national road, there are a filling station and tea-room to the left on the route south. Foreigners are often surrounded by a crowd of smiling children who will chatter away in Sesotho, oblivious to the fact that you have not the slightest idea what they are saying.

It is 38 km from Morija to Mafeteng. The tarred A2 national road passes through villages and out of the mountains into an area of wide plains fringed by flat-topped hills. Signs of a town become noticeable beyond the junction with the B42 gravel road to Tsita's Nek Pass. Houses crowd in along the road, and 50 m beyond Luma Pan visitors will enter the district capital of Mafeteng.

MAFETENG

Mafeteng is Sesotho for "one who passes by," the nickname of Emile Rolland, an interesting magistrate who once worked in the area and was popular with the locals. This busy trading town was an important staging post for colonising forces during the Basotho War. Mafeteng is often considered the gateway to Lesotho, and is of strategic importance to the military.

Orientation

Lying in an east-west direction, about 78 km south of Maseru, Mafeteng has two roads that will be of interest to visitors. The first enters town past Luma Pan in the north, then continues to the right through the central business district, before turning south and joining the A2 national road. The other enters the business district in the same way, but then branches to the west of the circle next to the radio masts. Route-marked as the A20 national road, it goes to the Van Rooyenshek border post with South Africa.

Visitors arriving from Maseru travel through an avenue of Lombardy poplar trees to a T-junction, in front of Kentucky Fried Chicken. To the left is the gravel B41 road into the eastern suburbs of Mafeteng. Turning right, visitors pass shopping centres and important government offices before reaching a circle surrounded by eucalyptus trees.

Important areas for visitors are situated along the main road through Mafeteng. This is where the post office, RLMP (police), shops, handicraft stalls, filling stations, banks and hotels are found. Go 20 m off this road in any direction, and you will find yourself in suburbs whose houses are a mixture of traditional and modern.

Finding your way around Mafeteng is easy if you begin and end tours at the same place; go in a large circle through the business district, suburbs, around the small hill which dominates the town, and then back onto the main road. Good places for reference points are the post office, the radio masts near the circle, and the Patsa Shopping Centre.

Information

Standard Chartered Bank is next to the Mafeteng Furniture Centre, on the main road through town; Barclays Bank is in a shopping complex across the road from Pep clothing store. In the same centre as Barclays is Likhoele Same-Day Dry Cleaners. They are quick and cheap, and laundry taken in before 09h00 can be collected at midday.

The Passport Office is in a dilapidated building across from the Patsa Shopping Centre. Trying to get any official documents in Mafeteng is a waste of time; most queries – even the non-existent price of a visa – are referred to Maseru, and you will have to wait at least two hours before an answer is received. Few of the clerks speak English, and the apathy in the office encourages most foreigners to try Maseru instead.

The RLMP (police) and post office are east of the Trade Centre, along the main road. To get to the police, turn in at the low sandstone building that has animal trophies hanging on the outside walls. Turn right at the trophies, go through the hedge and turn right onto the wooden veranda.

Though small, the post office is usually hectic –particularly at month-end – and has only a few tellers who take turns at serving the customers. You can expect a long wait. Poste restante is available at Mafeteng and telephone calls to South Africa are instant.

Visitors using public transport will be dropped off at the bus and minibus taxi stop, behind the abandoned stadium near the centre of Mafeteng. Transport going in either direction arrives at and departs from the same place. This is one of the busiest depots in Lesotho, and even visitors not using public transport should spend time walking among the travellers. Bus passengers in Lesotho carry the most unusual forms of luggage: chickens, the odd sheep or goat, food, alcohol, blankets and sometimes even suitcases.

Hitchhiking out of Mafeteng takes some effort: hikers must walk to the edges of the sprawling suburbs before they start hitching.

There are numerous filling stations in Mafeteng, most of them being at the northern entrance to town. They are located on both sides of the A2, just beyond the avenue of trees that passes Luma Pan. Some may be difficult to recognise if you are looking for a signboard – they don't have any, and the only indication is the row of minibus taxis filling up.

Things to see

Mafeteng is a trading centre; there is not much for visitors to see, but what is available is worth tracking down. Visitors with their own transport can leave their vehicles at the RLMP (police). Go to the RLMP traffic office to the left of the main charge office. It has happened that visitors who left their vehicles outside one of the hotels, having been guaranteed security, returned to find their vehicle broken into. Motorcyclists and cyclists should request that their belongings be kept inside the charge office.

British War Memorial

Erected by their Cape Mounted Rifles comrades, this forgotten memorial pays silent homage to the men who died so far from home, during the 1880–81 Basotho War. A sad place full of memories, the site is difficult to find even with your own transport. Few of the locals know of the memorial and visitors will have to rely on their own initiative to find it. Go to the circle at the western end of Mafeteng, and take the A20 national road towards Van Rooyenshek border post. Continue through the trees as far as the St John's Primary School sign. Turn onto the gravel at the large agricultural equipment yard, past the red-tile-roofed house on the left. About 20 m north of the line of tin shacks is a track to the right. The crumbling dry-stone walls mark the neglected War Memorial. The rusted iron gate doesn't open and visitors will have to clamber over the sandstone boulders to get in. Most of the headstones are difficult to read in the long grass, but the memorial itself stands out clearly. There are fading lists of names of the fallen soldiers, and in the silence the futility of it all becomes horrifyingly obvious.

Apart from the memorial, there is little to see in Mafeteng. But a walk through the town is interesting, and gives visitors an insight into the lives of the southern Basotho. Around the memorial is an area of modern houses, and the soccer stadium. Soccer matches are held on Sunday afternoons and visitors should try to see one of these rural African soccer games. East of the stadium the track joins a busy suburban road that travels among houses with beautiful gardens and guard dogs. One block south from the track is a gravel road that skirts houses before dipping into a polluted swamp, where the telephone and electricity lines are low enough to touch. Go through an alley between a red-bricked building and fenced-in shack, then onto the main road near Pep Stores.

A more enlightening route can be taken by walking from the bus depot on the B41 road, west for about 100 m; then begin to circle back over the small hill that is populated by beer brewers, cannabis merchants and dubious but fascinating Basotho restaurants. Keep the business district to the right and below you. Follow the path which goes past the town's water supply, through the trees overlooking the RLMP station. This path exits at the church on the main road, in the southern suburbs of Mafeteng. By continuing north on the road, you will come to the circle at the western end of the Trade Centre shopping complex.

Places to stay

With two hotels, Mafeteng gives visitors a choice of accommodation. It is inadvisable to camp near Mafeteng. With the strong police and military presence you can be sure of being hassled and told to move on, "Tsamaya."

Golden Hotel (medium–high tariff)

Located on the road from Maseru, past Luma Pan, this hotel is still new. A bit austere, the Golden Hotel is functional and comfortable. The manager is helpful and can arrange an expensive guide to the War Memorial. Accommodation is in 17 rooms, all with bathroom and television. The tariff is decided on the manager's interpretation of comfort; this can lead to some interesting negotiating. Budget travellers should make use of the cheap rooms with three or four beds crammed into them. Top-priced rooms have heaters and guests are served afternoon and morning tea. The tariff does not include meals, but visitors can eat in the usually empty dining room. There is a set breakfast and a verbal menu for lunch and dinner. The busy public bar is a good place to meet locals, and foreigners will not be left alone for long before people start coming over to talk. For visitors who would prefer a relaxing drink, the dark private bar, inside the hotel, stays quiet until about 19h30, when the overflow from the public bar spills into it. Horseriding and hiking are available during summer, and the swimming pool will soon be renovated. Outside the hotel is a hall in which movies are shown on Sunday; enquire from the receptionist what is showing. The hall is always full on movie day and you may have to sit on the floor. Do not expect to hear much of the film: most of the Basotho viewers will be loudly running their own commentaries. It is an experience, though, and you will have made some new friends before the end of the show. From the swimming pool there is a view across Luma Pan, and visitors can walk around the pan. Reservations are necessary at the hotel and guests should book at least three weeks in advance.

Address: Golden Hotel, P.O. Box 36, Mafeteng, 900, Lesotho
Telephone: (09266) 700566

Hotel Mafeteng (medium–high tariff)

To find the Hotel Mafeteng, take the road north, across from the Trade Centre in the business district. About 100 m further, on the right, is a large "Disco" sign within the hotel grounds, which lie behind security walls. The Hotel Mafeteng is very popular with locals. It is run down and seldom full of guests; the amenities are used mostly by the people who live in Mafeteng. The accommodation tariff is graded according to number of beds in the room: anything from one to four beds. Guests are accommodated in 27 rooms, all with bathroom; 15 rooms have television. Rooms are both in the hotel complex and in attractive rondavels in the garden. The tariff does not include meals, but visitors can order food in the hotel dining room from an à la carte menu. There are three bars: a private bar within the hotel, a crowded public bar and the disco-bar on Friday and Saturday evenings. The hotel manager is able to arrange horseriding and fishing trips in the area – he should be asked at least 24 hours before you intend going out. A conference hall is also located on site, as are a swimming pool and fuel facilities.

There is little to choose between the two hotels, but visitors who enjoy some night entertainment should try the Hotel Mafeteng – the disco really raves over weekends, gets crowded and goes on into the early hours.

Address: Hotel Mafeteng, The Manager, P.O. Box 109, Mafeteng, 900, Lesotho
Telephone: (09266) 700236

Camping (free)

Camping is not advised, but if you have no alternative, take the B41 road east. Continue for about 2 km to where the suburbs of Mafeteng give way to traditional villages. You can safely camp at any of the villages, and if you ask the headman, he will look after your belongings while you go to Mafeteng or into the surrounding countryside. The settlement of Likhoele, at which campers can expect wonderful treatment, is 8 km out of town. The villagers are friendly and fascinated by foreign campers and usually invite you to share their food at one of the village elders' homes. It is common courtesy to offer some of your own food, which can be added to the meal.

Places to eat

Mafeteng has many places where visitors can eat. Food ranges from à la carte menus to street-side snacks, and even vegetarians will find it easy to get a meal in Mafeteng. Unfortunately most visitors staying at the hotels take their meals in one of the dining rooms, and miss out on the experience of eating with the locals. It must be stressed, however, that travellers with weak stomachs should avoid the local fare and keep to hotel meals. The dining room of the Golden Hotel offers diners either an à la carte menu which is recited by the waitress or, over weekends, the day's special. Meals at the Golden Hotel are expensive and the service is atrocious, but it is quiet and a select wine list is available. The Hotel Mafeteng has a busy dining room with good service and a wider selection of meals. There are also daily specials available, and vegetarians can ask the manager for the vegetarian platter (which is not mentioned on the menu). Breakfasts are available at both hotels, and at the Hotel Mafeteng there are usually several travelling salespeople, with whom hitchhikers can find a lift.

In the central business district is Le Joint Restaurant, across from the Lesotho Urban Upgrading Project. A comprehensive à la carte menu is available, and diners have the choice of eating traditional or Western meals. Prices are reasonable and there is a warm, friendly atmosphere in the restaurant. This is another place where vegetarians will find suitable meals. Tell the manager when you enter the restaurant, and he will adapt the menu to accommodate you.

During the week, street vendors are a common site along the main road, and travellers have the opportunity of trying some of the freshly cooked local delicacies: roasted corn on the cob, mutton with curry sauce, hot brown bread dipped into a fiery chicken stew. Fresh fruit and vegetables are also on sale at these street stalls, as are sweets and packets of bright orange coloured crisps.

There are many Basotho restaurants and pubs in the southern and eastern suburbs of Mafeteng and, for budget travellers, are worth investigating. Well known and always full is the restaurant in the open area at the minibus taxi rank. For fast-food meals, try the Kentucky Fried Chicken near the bus depot. Further west up the main street, tasty food can be bought at J.R. Central Café, which also caters for Muslim visitors. South, past the circle, a basic Basotho meal can be eaten at the Square Meals shop.

Things to buy

The choice of handicrafts is limited, but there are a few places where visitors can find traditional Basotho goods for sale. There are no fixed prices, except at Fraser's Store, and visitors are expected to bargain good-humouredly for what they want to purchase.

At the Pii Hair Salon, behind the Passport Office, visitors can buy large, beautifully crafted handmade bed spreads. These are colourful, and some depict rural Basotho life. The assistant in the shop will also show you a number of Basotho-wool jerseys, which have been made locally. Prices start off high, but are suggested with a definite mischievous glint in the seller's eyes. A good starting point for a visitor is half of what has been asked. This usually results in raucous laughter, and then, with boundaries having been set, the real bargaining begins.

Fraser's Store next to the Hotel Mafeteng has a few Basotho blankets and crafts for sale. But because the shop is so close to a tourist hotel, prices are expensive.

Traditional trinkets can be bought from some of the hawkers, but they are made of inferior materials and are not worth their price.

South of Mafeteng the A2 national road continues to cross valleys, until about 18 km from Mafeteng it passes through the mission village of Siloe before swinging east towards the mountains. It continues through the villages of Molisane and Tsoloane before climbing a hill to the village of Ha Makhate and the view-point over the Makhaleng river. From the view-point the road drops onto a wide plain, with the Thaba-Putsoa Mountain range rising to the east, and ever-widening grasslands to the south.

Across the river and 6 km from Mohale's Hoek is the B40 road to Tsepo village. By following this gravel road north-east for 48 km, visitors will arrive at the mission settlement of **Masemouse**. Getting there for travellers without their own transport can take time, as there are few vehicles using this road, so you might as well start walking. Eventually some form of transport will come along, and if the driver is a Basotho, he will stop and offer you a ride.

Dominating the village is the highest mountain in southern Lesotho, Thaba Putsoa (2 908 m), meaning the "purple mountain". This peak can be climbed from base to summit in about three to four hours of fairly strenuous walking. And you can expect to take roughly two and a half to three hours for the descent back into the valley. Ask the Father at the mission for a guide; he will give you one of the children who drift around the church grounds. The view from the summit ridge is breathtaking: flatter regions to the west and south, and rising mountain ranges to the east and north.

Accommodation can sometimes be found at the mission and a tent-pitch is always available. There is usually also a bucket of hot water for washing.

Continuing along the A2 from the B40 T-junction, travellers will be able to see Mohale's Hoek to the south. The hills close in around the road, and slopes give way to sandstone cliffs with flat tops. On the plateau summits of these hills, reforestation projects are in progress and conifers can be seen growing. The western entrance to the district capital town of Mohale's Hoek is through a portal in a barrier of sandstone. Lombardy poplar trees line the road up a rise into the western area of town.

MOHALE'S HOEK

Eager to have peace with the monarchy in England, Chief Mohale (a brother of Moshoeshoe the Great) gave this valley to the British in 1884. The original settlement was more a garrison than a district centre, and little remains apart from a few crumbling walls and decaying buildings. The origins of the town would not be obvious to many visitors. Mohale's Hoek is a pleasant town surrounded by exotic trees and dry hills.

Orientation

Mohale's Hoek is fascinating in that it has street names that are legible and accurate. The most relevant areas for visitors are along the main road which runs through the business district –Mafoso Road. Here you will find the banks, RLMP (police), many shops and access to the bus and minibus taxi depot.

A starting point from which to explore the town is the RLMP station on the corner of Mafoso Road and the A2 national road. The Officer Commanding is a friendly woman who has overcome the most incredible obstacles to become one of the few female two-star majors in the male-dominated Royal Lesotho Mounted Police. You are permitted to leave your vehicle at the RLMP station, and will be given a constable to help unload your belongings into an office which will be locked.

To the north of the RLMP station is the Maluti Ring Road, where the hotel, a bank, hospital and post office are located. To the east of the RLMP station, the A2 winds out towards Moyeni.

It is difficult to get lost in Mohale's Hoek; on a slope overlooking town, in large white stones, is the name: Mohale's Hoek. It can be seen from virtually every part of town and is an excellent landmark while you walk around the alleys, roads and old buildings.

Information

The post office in Mohale's Hoek is on the Maluti Ring Road, about 50 m from the T-junction with the A2. Look for the radio masts behind the post office. Appearing abandoned, the post office is efficient. It is easy to make telephone calls to South Africa, there is a reliable poste restante service and most of the staff are cordial. A short-cut back into the central business district can be taken by continuing south along the gravel road that passes the Home Centre and exits near the RLMP station.

Both Standard Chartered Bank and Barclays Bank are in Mafoso Road. Standard Chartered is next to Mohale's Hoek Wholesalers, while Barclays is across from the RLMP station. The Lesotho Bank is on Maluti Ring Road in the Home Centre, near the post office. Standard and Barclays banks provide excellent service but high handling charges for transactions. Slower, more challenging and time-wasting, the Lesotho Bank is not recommended for travellers in a hurry who want to change large amounts – anything bigger than a $20 traveller's cheque.

Medical treatment is available at Sepetlele Hospital in Hospital Road, off Maluti Ring Road. As you enter Maluti Ring Road look for the sign indicating the Rural Health Services Project. Unless on the verge of death, or prepared to pay another patient in the line a bribe, you can expect a long wait, which admittedly ends in good medical attention.

Fuel is available from the Shell Mohale's Hoek Filling Station on the A2 national road. For visitors using public transport, there is an area of organised chaos that is the terminal. From the RLMP station walk up Mafoso Road to Fraser's Supermarket, turn left into the narrow alley, continue past Scott's Shoes and Squires Store into the open area that is the bus depot. Minibus taxis line either side of Mafoso Road, from in front of Standard Chartered Bank to the top end of town. Tenacity and patience are needed to find transport going your way. Destination names on scroll-boards are unreliable and travellers must walk around asking drivers their routes.

Hitchhiking from Mohale's Hoek first involves a 4 km minibus taxi or bus ride to the A18 national road towards the border post at Makhaleng Bridge. Walk further along the A2 road. From here, hitching a lift south is easy; there are many vehicles using this road in either direction. And, although the large trucks may just try to bowl you over in a rush of air as they pass, most cars stop – even if it looks as though they have not an inch more space available.

Things to see

Most of the interesting sites around Mohale's Hoek are not in town, and require some walking to reach. The town itself is condensed into a small area but the suburbs are spread out.

About 20 km from Mohale's Hoek, off the B39 road, are some Bushmen paintings and what are alleged to be dinosaur footprints. Take the A2 national road east out of Mohale's Hoek. Continue along this road for 9 km before turning onto the gravel B39 road. From the T-junction, drive 11 km to the Maphutseng river. Leave your vehicle at the shepherd's hut and follow the path across the road into the hills. The paintings are scattered in the cliffs and shallow caves. Various paths crisscross the hills and it takes strenuous walking to reach the paintings.

Herdboys will show you what looks like erosion marks on the stone slabs in the lower part of the valley – they will say that the marks are dinosaur footprints and then demand money for guiding you.

Before entering Mohale's Hoek from the north, visitors will notice sandstone cliffs along the A2 national road. Many of the caves and overhangs in these cliffs have Bushmen paintings which, being difficult to reach, are seldom visited by travellers. These paintings are well preserved and have some mystical symbols not found in other areas of Lesotho.

There is a local legend that tells of a spirit-filled, petrified forest in one of the valleys near Mohale's Hoek. Apparently a few of the locals know where the forest is, but I followed a number of guaranteed directions, and after four hours of exhausting searching gave up.

A walk around Mohale's Hoek allows visitors an interesting view into a Third-World centre rapidly becoming modernised. There are no traditional shops in the main street; most of the shops are typical city stores found anywhere in the world. Even many of the street hawkers have taken to selling music cassettes, sunglasses and luminous green combs. If you are determined for a sight of traditional Mohale's Hoek you will have to hunt around the bus terminal and up into the traditional villages in the hills. Mohale's Hoek is rapidly becoming like any First-World town in South Africa, and the traditional lifestyle is fading further back into the hidden valleys along the Maphutseng river.

Places to stay

Mohale's Hoek has limited accommodation for visitors. There is only one hotel, and although expensive, it provides high quality accommodation. For budget travellers, there are numerous valleys and hills around the town where you can camp. Ask at any of the villages a few kilometres out of town. The people are friendly and delighted to have foreigners staying with them. If you are really desperate, speak to the Major at the RLMP; she is willing to let you sleep on the floor in one of the offices and will even provide you with washing facilities. She will be delighted to receive fresh fruit as a "thank you," which can be bought from street vendors around the bus depot.

Hotel Mount Maluti (high tariff)

Situated in a beautiful garden in a northern suburb of Mohale's Hoek, the Hotel Mount Maluti is gracious and serene. To get to the hotel, take the Maluti Ring Road from its T-junction with the A2 national road. Continue past the post office and Lesotho Bank, and past the turnoff to the hospital; about 100 m further, on the left, is the entrance. Owned by the Bothma family since 1950, this is one of the best known hotels in Lesotho. The management is capable and friendly, and has much useful information about the area and other regions of Lesotho.

Accommodation is in 35 rooms, all with radio and television that works. Of these 35 rooms, 20 are single and 15 double. Visitors should note that the tariff does not include meals – breakfast can be included by paying a higher rate. Nine of the rooms have showers, the rest bathrooms. There are two bars: one public and one private. A conference hall, swimming pool and tennis courts take up the rest of the grounds. The owners have managed to create a magnificent garden between the various buildings, and many visitors may feel as if they are in a fairyland rather than in Lesotho. Most of the guests at the hotel arrive for conferences or travelling on business, and the attention to their comfort is evident in the service that all guests receive. For visitors who have been travelling long, this is one hotel that should be tried. It offers a chance to have a good meal from the à la carte menu and relax while being pampered by well-trained staff. Prior reservations must be made (at least 30 days in advance). Families should make enquiries about the Family Plan, in which children under the age of 15, who share with adults, stay free.

Address: Hotel Mount Maluti, P.O. Box 10, Mohale's Hoek, 800, Lesotho
Telephone: (09266) 785224

Other places to stay (free or low tariff)

Mohale's Hoek offers visitors who arrive with tents an opportunity for staying with the tribal Basotho. Leave town and walk or drive into any of the surrounding valleys. By following the path that skirts the large stone Mohale's Hoek sign, and then crossing over into the next valley, visitors will come to a settlement of about 10 traditional stone and thatch huts. The headman at this village is fluent in English and has some interesting legends to tell. Ask him to take you to meet the local "sangoma" (medicine man), who lives alone higher in the hills. This ancient grey-haired shaman will recount stories, through the headman, of strange spiritual happenings in the area, of the Cosmic Tree that links heaven and earth and of the Oneness in everything. He will give you things to think about as you continue your journey through Lesotho and through life.

Places to eat

Mohale's Hoek has surprisingly few places where visitors can eat. There are street-side snacks available, but full meals are limited to the Hotel Mount Maluti and poorly prepared take-aways from Ken-Con Fast Foods, at the bus terminal.

The dining room at the Hotel Mount Maluti is a refuge from the chaos of town. There is a large menu, and specials are occasionally offered. Non-residents should book ahead for meals, and be certain to arrive on time. The menu caters for most tastes, and every effort will be made to accommodate vegetarians. Even diabetics can have special foods prepared.

Snacks and light meals can be bought from the street vendors around the bus terminal and minibus taxi rank. There are various choices, ranging from roasted mutton and porridge to fried chicken served with bread and a highly spiced sauce. Fresh fruit and vegetables are available.

Getting meals in the villages is never a problem, and although the food is usually boiled mutton and porridge, it is filling. Offer to contribute something to the meal, such as fresh vegetables or tinned food.

The Feeling Good Restaurant, near Pep Stores, has a menu of mostly Basotho-style meals, but the food is cheap and the beer always ice-cold. Most of the diners are travellers waiting for their public transport. The restaurant is dirty and noisy, but if you can overlook that, it is a great place to meet locals and spend a while talking about their culture and concerns for the future.

Things to buy

Mohale's Hoek is not geared for visitors in search of curios. Items of interest to tourists are limited to a few trinkets and the odd blanket or jersey.

For handmade wooden statues, keyholders and simple furniture, try the green shack behind the bus terminal. Go through the bus area to the opening between the buildings, near Ken-Con Fast Foods. The carpenter is a talented young man who will make to order virtually anything out of wood. Small objects will be made the same day, but allow a few days for furniture or larger statues. All prices are negotiable, and are decided more on your eagerness to purchase an object than on its true value.

Fraser's Supermarket, Pep Stores, Squires and the wholesaler on Mafoso Road all have blankets for sale but many of them are not manufactured in Lesotho.

Jerseys and shawls can be purchased, but to find them takes effort. The women who sell in the informal sector, outside Scott's Shoes and Squires, can be approached. Although they themselves do not have these items for sale, they will call the ubiquitous children and get them to take you to one of the nearby villages, to the east of Mohale's Hoek. Here, many of the old women knit jerseys and the occasional shawl. The beauty of these village products is that they are not made with tourists in mind, but are rather intended for locals. These jerseys lack the finesse and high price of tourist goods; they are made from scratchy Basotho wool and coloured with natural dyes.

Leaving Mohale's Hoek to travel further south, visitors follow the A2 national road east through a small forest. About 4 km from town the road turns south and passes through changing terrain. To the south the hills give way to the wide valleys of South Africa, while to the east and north the hills become mountains.

Once across the Maphutseng and Mekaling rivers, travellers will find themselves passing through steep valleys and narrow canyons. Severe soil erosion is rapidly turning this area into a mass of deep dongas and naked hillsides. There are few animals around and grass is limited to the river banks, while hardy heather clings to the higher summits.

About 36 km south, along the tarred road from Mohale's Hoek, the road crosses the Seaka bridge over the Orange/Sengu river, and then climbs past an irrigation scheme. Run with foreign aid, this agricultural project is a model for other irrigation schemes in southern Lesotho. The site foreman speaks good English and is willing to take interested visitors on a tour. Water is pumped up from the Orange river via large lateral-line pipes to the irrigation project. It is hoped that through carefully controlled evaporation measurements, soil temperature records and plant growth monitors, this project will raise the level of sustainable agriculture in this part of Lesotho. Many of the agricultural advisors in Lesotho try to instil the need for a balanced "permaculture" type of production. Where monoculture had been the norm, visitors will be able to see that now different crops are being tried, so as to increase the potential of the soil and consequently the profitability of each hectare.

Across the bridge, the road changes its course from south to east, into a mountainous region. There are terraced hillsides along this route, and the locals make full use of every available piece of flat land for cultivation. They even try growing crops on river banks, which are prone to floods. This has however reduced the holding capacity of the soil and resulted in erosion scars around many of the rivers.

A gravel road turns right, 6 km from the Seaka bridge, and goes south-west to Tele Bridge border post with South Africa, 10 km away.

Travellers may notice the change in temperature as they enter the forested hills around Moyeni (Quthing): it is much warmer in this region of Lesotho. The road winds alongside the Qomoqomong river, through a gorge filled with exotic conifers, and down to the turnoff for Moyeni (Quthing).

MOYENI (QUTHING)

Meaning "place of the wind," Moyeni is another of the sites chosen by the British as an administrative centre. It remained the centre for the Quthing district for three years – until the Gun War of 1880 – then was abandoned by the embattled British. Later, however, after the conclusion of the war, it was resettled and more buildings were added. The original buildings of the British Administration can still be seen, and now house the Industrial Training School outside Moyeni.

Orientation

Moyeni lies 2 km off the A2 national road from Mohale's Hoek. Entering town, visitors pass through Lower Moyeni, where most of the shops, the market, public transport and fuel are found. The tarred road then climbs to a bend and up a steep hill to Upper Moyeni, where you can find the bank, RLMP (police), hospital and government offices.

Lower Moyeni lies in a valley above a bend in the Qomoqomong river. To the south are cliffs, and to the north the valley drops to an alluvial plain and the river. Upper Moyeni is draped across the spur of a hill. Most of this area is covered in conifer trees, and there are spectacular views to the mountains. The area between the two parts of town is a mixture of traditional and modern suburbs. Upper Moyeni is the developing section, while Lower Moyeni has kept its rural atmosphere.

As there is only one tarred road linking the sections of town, finding your way is easy. There is no need to follow the road: many paths take short-cuts between Upper and Lower Moyeni. Lower Moyeni lies in an east-west direction, and Upper Moyeni north-south, which means that visitors exploring the alleys and suburbs are always in sight of either part of town.

If you are venturing out into the surrounding areas, all you need to ask to get back into town is, "Upi Quthing?" (Where is Quthing/Moyeni?). Unusual for Basothos, the locals will not try and give you short-cut routes through forests, rivers and villages, but instead will direct you on the simplest route back to the A2 national road.

Information

Banks are in Upper Moyeni. Go about 60 m past Fraser's Store on the left when you have entered Upper Moyeni. Standard Chartered Bank, Lesotho Bank and the Agricultural Bank are near one another, to the east of the grassy circle. This circle with its tattered military flag is the hub around which the business area of Upper Moyeni is built. Service at the banks is slow, and changing hard foreign currency into local cash is impossible. Even traveller's cheques can be a problem. If you need to cash traveller's cheques, try the Standard Chartered Bank before the others. The Lesotho Bank is famous for giving tourists small change; if you are changing $50 this can mean that your hand luggage will end up bulging with coins and weighing quite a few kilograms.

At M. Fokotsane and Sons General Dealer, near the banks, same-day laundry can be done. The washing is thorough, but you will need to replace a few smashed buttons.

The RLMP station is also in the same area, behind a security fence. This station has the friendliest troopers in Lesotho, and is a good place to leave your vehicle if you do not intend staying in Moyeni.

Government offices and the post office are across from the RLMP station. This is a quiet, friendly backwater post office. The staff are amiable and enjoy having long conversations with foreigners. If the telephone lines are operational, a telephone call can be made instantly to any destination in Lesotho. International calls require a booking through Maseru. Very few travellers use this post office and the arrival of one is something of an occasion. You will be offered a cup of tea while the staff ask a hundred questions without waiting for any answers – it becomes hilarious when mismatched questions and answers cause total confusion. Business usually concludes with one of the staff inviting you home for a meal.

Lower Moyeni has the larger of the two business districts, and a number of important places are located here. Spares and minor repairs to cars, trucks, motorbikes and bicycles are available at Main Street Motors Workshop, just before the road climbs to Upper Moyeni. The mechanic is a graduate of the South African Transport Services Training School. He is capable, slow and cheap. For example, a puncture repair will cost you next to nothing, take three hours and look new when finished.

Across the road from the motor workshop is Atlantic Opticians. Having your eyes tested here is really a remarkable experience – visitors should try it.

Further west is the fuel filling station, outside Lower Moyeni Store. Next to it is the bus and minibus taxi terminal. There is no order here, and most of the time the road is blocked with traffic. The buses and minibus taxis for western Lesotho park on both sides of the main road, while the bus for Sehlabathebe waits outside the Lepule Trading Store. Getting a minibus taxi out of Moyeni to either destination is relatively simple: ask any of the street vendors sitting outside Lower Moyeni Store; they usually send someone to take you to the vehicle.

Hitchhikers leaving Moyeni should walk about 2 km out of town, onto the A2 national road. In this way they will be able to get lifts with traffic going in either direction.

Quthing Hospital is undergoing reconstruction, which will make it compare favourably with any Maseru hospital. Located in Upper Moyeni, the hospital is difficult to see from the main road. When you reach the abandoned church, across from the Orange River Hotel, turn right. This gravel road goes past the back of the RLMP station and ends at the Quthing Hospital. Medical attention is difficult to find at the hospital, as visitors have to walk around unmarked buildings looking for the right room. Stop any nurse who walks past and ask her to take you to a particular building or to the reception office.

Things to see

Moyeni is a good location from which to visit a number of interesting local sites. Most places lie a few kilometres outside town and require some walking. Although a vehicle can be used to get near the sites, the final stretch must be done on foot. The paths to the sites are well used, and on most days visitors will encounter other people on them.

Masitise cave house

To reach this site, visitors will have to travel back along the A2 national road towards the Seaka bridge. About 5 km west of Lower Moyeni the road climbs a low hill. On the crest of the hill is a signboard indicating the direction to Masitise Primary School. Turn left onto the gravel track and follow it through the cultivated fields. There is a rocky drop to an almost impassable gateway and then the track leads up to the school buildings. Visitors are not allowed to explore the area alone, and must get permission from the school headmaster. His house is the stone and thatch one with the impressive garden, about 50 m behind and to the left of the school buildings. He has the keys to the old mission and cave dwelling, and also acts as a guide.

Visitors will first pass the church, which was built in 1883 and is filled to capacity during Easter celebrations. Then on through a gate and past the orange house, also built in 1883. This was the second home, after the cave dwelling, of the first missionary to the area, the Reverend D.F. Ellenberger from Switzerland. The barn-like mud building, which is now a storeroom, originally housed the press for the mission's tracts. From here a narrow path turns into the forest and begins to climb the hill. On a level piece of land, under a brooding sandstone overhang, is the cave house. An inscription on the cliff names the best known of its inhabitants, the Reverend D.F. Ellenberger. Vandalised and neglected, the cave house still evokes memories of history. The windows are barred and cemented, as is the front door. Visitors enter between what was once the kitchen and dining room. The house is low roofed and hints at hardship. Dusty old Bibles and sheet music with lyrics in Tswana are on display, as are original drawings and faded photographs. In the bedroom is a small paleo-zoology collection and what, at first, may look like a pile of stones. The son of the Reverend Ellenberger was taught, by the herdboy who first lived in the cave while looking after Chief Moorosi's cattle, how to arrange this pile of stones so that music could be played on them – the secret is now forgotten, but it is fun trying to reconstruct the musical stones.

At the end of the forest path back to the main buildings, visitors will see the ruins of a building to the left, among trees. This was the original church hall. Between the press house and the round stone rondavel stands a wild olive tree reputedly planted by the Reverend Ellenberger over 100 years ago. It is possible to walk around inside the old house (remind the headmaster to take his key), which is still used by the priest from Morija whenever he comes to inspect this outpost of his parish.

Bushmen paintings

There are numerous paintings in the caves scattered about the surroundings of Moyeni. Those near the cave house have been vandalised, and youngsters have added their own graffiti to the ancient painted stories. But a strenuous hike to the cliffs across the Qomoqomong river will take you to a series of cliffs with numerous shallow caves, many of which have excellent Bushmen paintings.

The official tourist paintings can be seen about 10 km to the east of Moyeni. At the top end of Lower Moyeni, where the road bends to climb to Upper Moyeni, a road continues straight on past the sign indicating the Mountain Side Hotel. Continue to the end of the road at the village of Qomoqomong. On the western hill, above the village, is a difficult path up to the summit of the hill. Beyond this hill, in the cliffs, are caves with well-preserved paintings. Local children will offer to act as guides.

Dinosaur footprints

Always a great attraction, the dinosaur footprints can be seen to the west of Lower Moyeni. At the T-junction, where the road to Moyeni joins the A2, turn left and proceed for about 100 m. Below the Leloalang Industrial Training School, turn right and go down the slope to the river. A short walk along the opposite river bank, in either direction, will take you to fossilised footprints. Those to the east, near the bend in the river, are particularly well preserved. Those in the river bed and above the bank, to the west, are difficult to see.

About 12 km further up the Qomoqomong river is another set of seldom seen dinosaur footprints. Follow the river upstream and ask the shepherds at the second little waterfall you come across after leaving the village of Qomoqomong. This is a demanding hike, and unless you start out early you will have to camp or sleep at one of the villages along the river.

Other sights

A small European cemetery is located across from the closed church, on the main road into Upper Moyeni. Overgrown and hidden among trees, this cemetery is seldom visited. Most of the headstones name a long line of British and American aid-workers who had come to assist the Basotho in their quest for progress and modernisation.

West along the A2 national road is the site of the first watermill constructed in Lesotho. The site now houses the Leloalang Industrial Training School, which visitors may view. Contact someone in the Mechanical Faculty, which is in the first building on the left past the Leloalang School entrance. You will be taken through the old buildings and shown the various vocational skills being taught, as well as the remains of the watermill. Not surprisingly, the Basotho have neglected all British historical sites.

Places to stay

Accommodation in Moyeni is limited and expensive, but visitors arriving with their own tents will find hundreds of pitches around Upper Moyeni and in the valleys. Two hotels serve the tourist trade: the more comfortable but expensive Orange River Hotel, and the basic but cheaper Mountain Side Hotel.

Orange River Hotel (high tariff)

This hotel is in Upper Moyeni, on the side of a hill overlooking the Qomoqomong river. Take the main road through Lower Moyeni and go up to the tree-lined avenue just before Upper Moyeni. At the radio masts, turn left onto a gravel track which skirts the hotel's public bar and ends at the steps above the reception office.

The first thing that strikes most visitors is the faded opulence of the hotel. Underfloor heating, chandeliers and plush furniture create a good impression. But the care that must have once been lavished on this hotel is gone. Neither of the receptionists speaks English, and the manager, courteous but abrupt, openly admits to preferring guests who arrive with Lesotho Government Pay Orders. He claims that foreign guests regularly steal from the rooms; a German aid-sponsored teacher, he says, recently stole the whole shower unit off the bathroom wall. Still, the hotel has uninterrupted views of the countryside and provides good access to many isolated points of interest.

The high tariff covers room only, but guests can eat in the dining room and order drinks from the residents' bar. Accommodation is provided in 12 rooms in the hotel building and in another four rooms in the thatched rondavels in the hotel grounds. All rooms in the hotel building have en suite bathroom, telephone and radio, plus underfloor heating. During winter the heating is enjoyable, but in summer it is also kept on, and as the heat-adjuster in most of the rooms does not work, it can become uncomfortable. Rondavel guests have to share a communal bathroom. There are television sets in the 12 hotel rooms, but the hotel's video channel is the only viewing on offer.

A deposit is required before a guest is given a room key –according to the manager, many of the foreign guests leave without paying their bill (''especially teachers from the villages on the road to Qacha's Nek''). Credit cards are not accepted, nor are personal or even company cheques.

Horseriding can be arranged free of charge at the RLMP (police). There is excellent fishing in the river, but guests must bring their own tackle and obtain a licence from: The Fisheries Officer, Ministry of Agriculture, P.O. Box 24, Maseru, 100, Lesotho.

The swimming pool is empty and will remain so until funds are found to replace the mosaic. Guided trips to see Bushmen paintings and dinosaur footprints can be arranged through the hotel manager, but only on summer mornings. Reservations are necessary.

Address: Orange River Hotel, The Reservations Manager, P.O. Box 37, Moyeni (Quthing), 700, Lesotho
Telephone: (09266) 750252

Other accommodation

Along the gravel road from Lower Moyeni to the village of Qomoqomong is the Mountain Side Hotel (medium tariff). Travellers seldom use this hotel unless in dire need, and it is not recommended for the safety-conscious or squeamish. The number of beds or rooms available fluctuates, and you will have to take whatever is given. One hardened traveller who slept here, having made his way overland from Italy, said it was the worst place for bugs he had encountered in 18 months of travelling through Africa. Lack of security has been a problem, as have the forceful locals who crowd the one bar.

Budget visitors should try the Villa Maria Roman Catholic Mission (small donation), which is off the A2 national road, about 500 m west of the Leloalang Industrial Training School. The mission workers are friendly and will offer you a bed if there is one, and washing facilities. If no bed is available, visitors can camp in the mission grounds and use the washing facilities. You will even be invited to partake of community meals.

Camping (free)

Many of the hills around Moyeni are forested, and travellers can erect a tent virtually anywhere. If you are uncertain who the local chief is, ask the Police Captain, at the RLMP station in Upper Moyeni, for a letter in Sesotho permitting you to camp in the area under his jurisdiction. Take care, however, if you decide to camp near the suburbs of town. It is better to go up into one of the valleys extending from Upper Moyeni. These valleys have fragrant forests, meadows full of wild flowers, clean streams and few people. It is safe to leave your tent and go walking around the hills. Your only observers will be herdboys who smile and raise a hand in greeting as you pass.

Places to eat

Moyeni has no formal restaurants other than the dining room of the Orange River Hotel. But visitors have a large choice of snacks and local food from the street vendors.

The dining room of the Orange River Hotel offers guests magnificent views across the mountains. There is a set menu. Vegetarians have no choice but to order a complete dish, then eat only the boiled vegetables. Meals are enormous and visitors seldom finish everything on the set menu. The advantage of eating at the hotel is that the kitchen is clean and chefs are well trained. Apart from the overboiled vegetables, the food is well prepared, tasty and artistically presented.

Out on the streets, visitors have an opportunity of tasting traditional Basotho food. The market is behind the post office in Upper Moyeni, in a large tin shed. This is where fresh fruit and vegetables can be bought. However, it is in Lower Moyeni that meals and snacks can be had. Outside Lower Moyeni Store are many street vendors who sell fried "makwenya" dough cakes in brown paper. This bread-like food is excellent when eaten with spicy stewed chicken, which can be bought outside the Quthing Shopping Centre. The street vendors around the bus and minibus taxi terminal sell many different types of food, some interesting and tasty, such as stewed mutton with vegetables in a thick herb gravy; others bizarre and inedible to most foreigners, such as roasted sheep heads with mushrooms in the eye sockets and nostrils.

For alcohol, there is little to beat the experience of drinking at the popular Monyakeng Liquor Restaurant. From Lower Moyeni, take the path to the right of Main Street Motors. Go past the circular stone house and walk along the path that turns left up the hill. About 50 m further, on the left, is the liquor restaurant. Both traditional and Western beer is available. It is easy to lose track of time in the restaurant; there is a steady stream of men and women coming and going. At first they will be shocked to see a foreigner in the place, but soon someone will come over and begin talking. Expect to be the centre of a friendly crowd if you stay for more than one drink.

Things to buy

Moyeni is far from the tourist markets of Western Lesotho, and has little to offer for sale to visitors. Some locally handmade jerseys, shawls and car seat covers can be bought from the Liphakoe Mountain Woollens workshop in Upper Moyeni. The items are all beautifully made and their prices negotiable. To reach the workshop, go to the circle in Upper Moyeni and take the gravel road west, behind the post office. About 70 m down this road, to the left of the fresh produce market shed, is a track with a sign indicating the workshop.

To continue along the southern route, visitors must return to the A2 national road, then turn north along the A4 national road. Follow the signs to Fort Hartley, Mount Moorosi and Qacha's Nek.

The settlement of **Fort Hartley** is 12 km to the north. This village is named in honour of Surgeon-Major E.B. Hartley, who risked his life to rescue wounded soldiers during a Cape Mounted Rifles' abortive attack in 1879 on Chief Moorosi. For his valour in the incident, the Surgeon-Major was awarded the rare Victoria Cross. Although most road maps show fuel being available at Fort Hartley, it has not been for many years. No accommodation is available, and if you intend exploring the prehistorically rich area, you will have to camp and take your own food.

Beyond Fort Hartley the road, which has been following the course of the Orange river, rises to the village of Cutting Camp. The hills above the river are covered in thick vegetation, especially aloes which bear beautiful orange and yellow flowers. On the more barren slopes the Department of Forestry has started afforestation programmes using conifer trees. On every piece of level land the locals are cultivating crops – this is a rare insight into a rural culture's agricultural endeavour.

For 32 km the tarred road rises and drops, sometimes hugging steep hillsides hundreds of metres above the Orange river, sometimes snaking at water level in the thickly bushed valleys.

Finally the road drops to the historical town of **Mount Moorosi**. Dominating the town is the cliff-fringed fortress of one of Lesotho's fiercest chiefs. Chief Moorosi was a bandit, rustler and rebel. He moved his Baphuthi tribe into these highlands in the 1850s, crossing the massif of the Drakensberg from South Africa and setting up this impregnable outlaw hideout. He frequently led rustling parties into South Africa, where his exploits soon had the white farmers complaining. When, in 1877, the British made Moyeni the district capital, they attempted to subdue Moorosi by imprisoning his son Doda. Chief Moorosi coolly sent some of his bandits to liberate his son. This they did, and returned Doda to the mountain fortress. Repeatedly the British tried to capture Moorosi – going so far as to place a reward on his head, dead or alive.

After a campaign lasting nearly two years, the British gained the summit and attacked the fortress. What followed will forever be a black mark in Imperial Britain's history. Over 200 warriors and 300 women, children and old people were slaughtered by the victorious British. Among the dead was Chief Moorosi, whose head was cut off and publicly displayed.

Fuel is available in Mount Moorosi – the last until you reach Qacha's Nek, 135 km away. To get to the fuel pumps, go past the minibus taxi and bus rank in the middle of town along the A4, and turn right onto the gravel road that dips towards a small wood. There is a BP signboard at the turning. About 150 m further is Mitchell Bros. Trading Store, where fuel can be purchased.

Mitchell's Café prepares delicious fish and chips, and fiery hot curried chicken served with papad brown bread.

Visitors travelling by public transport should take one of the many minibus taxis that run between Moyeni and Mount Moorosi, or the daily bus that travels to Moyeni from Qacha's Nek.

From Mount Moorosi the road becomes both challenging and interesting. Visitors now enter an area of hairpin bends, steep ascents and precipitous descents. A few kilometres past Mount Moorosi the road climbs to the summit ridge of a range of mountains; 15 km further the tar is replaced by a good gravel surface. Beyond that, the steepest sections of the road are still tarred as far as **Mphaki**, where all tar ends.

Mphaki lies in a hollow along the upper Qhoali river. Tuesday is livestock sale day, and visitors should try to attend.

Beyond Mphaki the gravel road becomes a diabolical track, full of potholes, stones and sheer drops into the valleys below. Bikers and cyclists should be careful along this section of road, as the stones and ruts affect the balance of a bike. Continue across causeways and up what resembles a donga, but is in fact the road to **Sekake**.

There are foreign teachers in some of the schools around the post office village of Sekake. They are not too fond of visitors and will only grudgingly provide shelter, if you must sleep there. Most of the houses have well-tended gardens and red roofs. On the far side of town is the Southern Mountain Weavers workshop. Visitors can watch the crafters at work or browse among the handmade blankets, jerseys and carpets. Prices are fixed by the co-operative scheme, but bargaining is expected.

East of Sekake you will travel through cultivated lands to the Orange river. Visitors wanting to see Bushmen paintings should leave their transport at the road camp, where the road drops to the river bank, about 18 km from Sekake. Cross the river below the road camp and then walk west along the bank. In the cliffs along the river, for nearly 1 km, are shallow caves with paintings. Some are hidden behind bushes and in cracks of the cliffs. Not known along the tourist trail, many of these paintings have seldom been seen by visitors.

About 2 km from the road camp, the road passes through the village of **White Hill**. White Hill boasts the Lesotho Cash Store, feedsheds and possibly one of the tiniest post offices in the world. East of White Hill, the usual yellow colour of the gravel road changes to pink and sometimes white.

Where the road penetrates deeper into the mountains the locals have cut narrow terraces across the lower slopes. Another 11 km east the road becomes the A15 national road, which goes past the impressive cathedral at Hermitage Mission near Mpiti, and then through hills before entering the western side of Qacha's Nek.

QACHA'S NEK

Qacha's Nek is another of the outlaw centres that once flourished in southern and eastern Lesotho. The name means "hideout pass". By 1888 the British Administration had subjugated or killed most of the bandit leaders, and those who survived retreated into the mountains or into the Transkei. Determined not to let the survivors become as uncontrollable as they had at Mount Moorosi, the British established a district capital at Qacha's Nek and brought in a regiment of troops to enforce the law. Yet even today there is the hint of lawlessness about the town, and the RLMP's Stock Theft Unit remains one of the busiest in Lesotho.

Orientation

Qacha's Nek is 179 km from Moyeni, along what rates as the most scenic route in Lesotho. The town is built in a U-shape over two hills, which are separated by a shallow valley. The main business district of Qacha's Nek is located on the southern side of the town, about 1,5 km east of the tarred airstrip.

Most areas of interest to visitors are to be found along the southern side of this mountain town. This is where the bank, post office, RLMP (police), restaurants, fuel filling station, hotel, bus and minibus taxi depot, shops and some of the tourist attractions are located. The A15 national road is also the Qacha's Nek main road, and finding your way around town is simple if you keep to this main road which not only links the two sections of town, but also provides access to secondary roads.

The southern part of Qacha's Nek is built in a west-east direction, and lies draped over a hill. Northern Qacha's Nek is where the modern shopping centres are located. Visitors are able to see both sides of town from virtually any point in the area; the one exception is that the business districts are not visible from the airport or from the hotel just outside Qacha's Nek.

Information

Qacha's Nek has one of the busiest airports in Lesotho, and flying is the preferred method of transport for people arriving from Maseru. Although the drive from the capital leads through spectacular countryside, the effort and tenacity required to complete it are more than many people are prepared for. The airstrip is about 1,5 km west of town, and travellers hoping to board a flight should go to the airport buildings and wait near the fuel depot.

For visitors arriving by plane, the Nthatuoa Hotel is only about 100 m west, along the main road. There are numerous minibus taxis travelling this section of road, and you will have little trouble getting to town or the hotel.

Visitors travelling by public transport arrive in and depart from the central business district on the southern side of town. The buses and minibus taxis congregate outside the Vuku Zenzele Café and Restaurant, near the Qacha's Nek Shell Filling Station in the middle of town. Minibus taxi drivers in this region of Lesotho have a peculiarity not found elsewhere: they hang cowbells from the chassis of their vehicles, so that when they travel about they sound like frantic Swiss cows. Travellers need to ask the drivers their destinations, because some only do local trips while others make the long journeys to Mohale's Hoek or Maseru. There is one daily bus going further north-east, to Sehlabathebe National Park. You can safely assume that all other public transport is going south.

Where to start hitchhiking out of Qacha's Nek depends on your intended route. Hikers heading out of Lesotho need to walk to the border post east of town. Go to the circle, about 60 m from the Qacha's Nek Shell Filling Station. At the circle, take the right fork in the road, which goes through a tree-lined avenue and then up to the border post. Cross the Lesotho border and walk another 200 m to the Transkei border. On the Transkei side you will have to begin walking and hope that a lift will stop. This route out of Lesotho is possibly the worst for hitchhikers – vehicles are few and usually crowded with people and livestock.

Hitchhikers going further north should walk past the Nthatuoa Hotel and wait on the level stretch of road above the river. If your lift is going west, along the A4 national road, get out at the village of Mpiti and take the road to the right. You may as well start walking as there is seldom traffic along this route, but any vehicle there is with a Basotho driver, will usually stop for you

Fuel is available at Qacha's Nek Garage and Nthatuoa Restaurant, within 20 m of each other, in the southern section of Qacha's Nek. The post office and RLMP station are back to back, to the left of the circle in the southern business district. Turn left at the circle, go past the sheds and turn left into the open area outside the post office. The post office is not open at the times indicated outside, and it is best to get there between 09h30–11h30. Travellers who have tried to use this post office as a poste restante have been unsuccessful, and one Peace Corps volunteer worker waited eight months for a letter to be sent from Maseru to the poste restante in Qacha's Nek. Telephone calls are also difficult, as the lines pass over mountain ranges and through areas frequently lashed by storms.

The RLMP station is behind the post office and can be approached either through the gate to the left of the post office or by continuing east along the main road and turning into the main entrance about 50 m further on. Because Qacha's Nek is a border town, visitors will notice the many military and police personnel here. As are most paramilitary forces in Third World countries, they are belligerent and unhelpful, and any foreigner suspected of taking "sensitive" photographs will be taken to the crumbling RLMP station and interrogated. (South Africans need to be especially careful.)

Medical treatment is available at Machabeng Hospital. About 200 m east of the airport is a sign indicating Lesotho Milling; a few metres east, past the large generator, is a gravel road that leads to the hospital. Conditions at the hospital are primitive and cases involving surgery or trauma are transported by air to the nearest South African hospital.

The Lesotho Bank is outside Qacha's Nek, next to Lesotho Milling, west along the A15 national road. As at other rural banks in Lesotho, visitors should allow themselves at least two hours to exchange money. The staff are not used to cashing traveller's cheques, and visitors should make certain that they have received the correct amount when the transaction is completed. If there are any discrepancies, go directly to the bank manager and avoid getting into an argument with the clerks – this sometimes requires the patience of a saint.

Things to see

Lacking the historical landmarks found in other urban centres, Qacha's Nek does however have some points of interest for visitors. Most of these sites are accessible by vehicle, but visitors should rather leave their transport somewhere safe, such as at the hotel, and walk the roads and paths that wind their way between the two sections of town. For those who have decided on Qacha's Nek being their exit point from Lesotho, this is the last chance of mixing with the quiet and mysterious Basotho.

A good place from which to begin an exploratory tour of Qacha's Nek is the Nthatuoa Hotel, about 3 km west of town. Walk east along the gravel road that goes past the Qacha's Nek road maintenance camp and airport. At the top of the hill there is a level section which passes the school's sports fields – where the children insist on calling any white man "Father". Continue alongside the pasture lands of the agricultural co-operative, which is the design model for this area of Lesotho. Because most of the locals grow wheat or raise livestock, foreign aid programmes have poured money into teaching them how to plan, manage and care for their mountain farms. Beyond the co-operative the road rises to the Lesotho Bank and Lesotho Milling. Over the crest is a suburban area of modern block houses, then the road drops to cross high speed-humps and enter the town.

Visitors walking the streets of Qacha's Nek will hear a mixture of languages being spoken. With a chequered history that has seen a number of tribes influencing the area, Qacha's Nek has become an African version of cosmopolitan. Shy blanketed Basotho, larger more extrovert Zulus, Mapondos with their traditional vertical scars on the cheeks, Xhosas with their lilting clicking language and a sprinkling of Griquas and whites make Qacha's Nek an interesting mixture of architecture, customs, clothing and attitudes.

Turn left at the circle and go past the post office, RLMP station and old sandstone houses in large, beautiful rose gardens. Near the last colonial house on the right, on the hill, are some of the town's famous Californian redwood trees. These trees were planted over 50 years ago, and some are over 25 m tall. There are two versions of how they got here; both feature foreigners. The first story claims that American missionaries planted the trees when they arrived at the site in the 1940s. The other story has it that workers in a Canadian aid project planted the trees in an attempt to introduce forestry to the district. But whatever the truth, the tall trees lend a certain grandeur to this already captivating town.

The road continues around the cup of the U-shape. To the right is the craft centre, and to the left a forest of pine and other exotic trees. It is easy to forget that you are in Lesotho; Canada seems more likely – mountains, conifer forests, cascading streams and clear skies make Qacha's Nek very un-African.

Continuing from the forest, visitors pass a number of shops, bars and hair salons before coming to Pep Stores on the right. Across the valley to the east are the spires of St Joseph's church. In the gardens of this church visitors can view more Californian redwood trees. To walk to the church turn right between Pep Stores and the red-roofed livestock pen. Go down the hill, past the radio masts and another livestock yard, to the gravel road that twists through the forest to St Joseph's church. The trees are mixed in with other conifers, on the slope to the south of the church. Initially difficult to find among the other trees, the redwoods can be distinguished by their wider trunk and greater height.

Returning along the gravel road, travellers enter the northern business district of Qacha's Nek with its modern shopping centres. This is where the town's youth gather. There are a number of paths between the two sides of town, and visitors who do not mind more walking should take the path that drops to the stream, goes through the edge of the valley forest and then up to the RLMP station.

For a good view of Qacha's Nek, take the road towards the border post from the circle. At the second rondavel on the left, turn onto the path that goes up the hill. Follow the barbed-wire fence to the sandstone summit. There is a panorama of mountain ranges and valleys across both sides of Qacha's Nek. At the summit you will be on a level with the tallest redwoods overlooking the RLMP station and post office.

The area around Qacha's Nek is suitable for day hikes. Walkers should keep in mind though that this is a sensitive border area, and should avoid going on any path that heads east, into the disputed border territory.

About 7 km west of Qacha's Nek is the Hermitage Cathedral. Built in 1974 by Father Hammond (from Canada), the cathedral is unique in southern Lesotho. Visitors may tour the cathedral and its associated primary and high school. Before walking around the grounds, ask permission from the Father at the rectory. However, the staff prefer that visitors who intend seeing the cathedral complex contact them prior to arrival, so that a guide can be provided. Make arrangements through Mary Phatela, who works in the bar of the Nthatuoa Hotel.

Places to stay

Visitors wanting to stay in Qacha's Nek have four options from which to choose: Nthatuoa Hotel, St Joseph's, the Hermitage, and camping in one of the forests or near the river. If you go into the remote valleys, a campsite or traditional hut is available at most of the villages.

Nthatuoa Hotel (high tariff)

Used more by businesspeople than tourists, this splendid little hotel 3 km west of Qacha's Nek is a gem on the Lesotho hotel circuit. Set in a narrow riverine valley, the Nthatuoa Hotel is the perfect place from which to explore Qacha's Nek and the surrounding countryside. Visitors travelling through Lesotho will pass the hotel when going east to Qacha's Nek, while those entering from the Transkei will reach the hotel by going through the southern part of Qacha's Nek and the business district, then west past the airport.

The Nthatuoa is comfortable and well managed. The owners' attention to the least detail ensures cleanliness and a high standard of service.

According to the owners, "Our motto is that each guest's satisfaction is our livelihood." This attitude shows in the quality of what the hotel offers.

Guests are accommodated in three blocks, A, B and C, comprising 20 rooms. Each block has a different tariff, which depends on the number of furnishings in the rooms. All rooms have bathrooms; 12 have television, radio and battery-powered telephone. The A block is the most popular with budget travellers; each room has a small bathroom, a tiny bath and a bed. B block has bigger baths and bathrooms, and the rooms are more spacious, but they still have only single beds. Top of the range is C block. These rooms are the largest and most expensive, each with a radio, television, telephone, large double bed, electric blanket and full furnishings. But no matter which room you have chosen, or whether you have decided instead to camp in the grounds (for free), the quality of service remains high. Even campers can expect to be called in their tent at 07h30 and offered tea on a silver tray.

There is one bar, which serves both guests and locals. Contrary to the norm at many other hotels in Lesotho, the tariff at the Nthatuoa Hotel includes bed and breakfast. Lunch and dinner can be eaten in the high-ceilinged dining room.

Hotel staff can arrange pony-trekking, trout fishing and permits, hiking trails, guides and transport to view the Bushman paintings at St Francis Mission, 25 km to the north. They even go so far as to arrange for the hotel's driver and vehicle to take guests to points of interest around town and to the Hermitage, providing packed lunches for the trip. Guests who plan to stay at the hotel must make reservations at least 30 days ahead, and should confirm them by telegram 15 days before arrival.

Address: Nthatuoa Hotel, P.O. Box 167, Qacha's Nek, Lesotho
Telephone: (09266) 95260 or 95207

Other places to stay (free or donation)

Of the two missions, St Joseph's is the better: it lies within 1 km of Qacha's Nek, while the Hermitage is 7 km away. To get to St Joseph's, follow the road to the northern side of town, and at the end of the shopping centre take the right fork into the forested valley to the church. The Father will allow you to sleep in one of the empty outbuildings and will provide washing facilities.

You may also camp anywhere in the forest around the church. It can be a bit eerie in the forest at night, especially when there is a full moon.

It is a spiritual place, full of quiet strength and unusual harmony. To visitors who are trying to get in touch with their real selves, a night in this forest will reveal many truths. A contribution to the church is greatly appreciated.

At the Hermitage, guests will invariably be given a room, washing facilities and, if they arrive at the right time, a simple and filling meal. The priests and nuns at the Hermitage are friendly but somewhat removed from this plane, and what some visitors describe as aloofness, others call peace. At least one member of the Hermitage goes into Qacha's Nek daily, and visitors without transport can arrange a lift the previous evening. Leave a suitable donation, it makes things easier for those who come after you.

Camping is possible anywhere beyond the town limits, and there is something exciting about sleeping in the hills or villages where outlaws once hid with their loot and rebels laid plans late into the night. Avoid drinking the water from the streams: even the highest places have some sort of settlement with cattle and sheep. Snow covers most of the countryside around Qacha's Nek during winter and camping in the wilderness areas is then not recommended.

Places to eat

Qacha's Nek, like most border towns, has several places where visitors can buy food. Numerous street vendors sell snacks and light meals. Fresh fruit and vegetables can be difficult to find, but a good place to try is the Raohang market gardens on the U-shape bend in the road that links the two sides of Qacha's Nek.

Most visitors take their meals at the Nthatuoa Hotel, which has an extensive menu and a good selection of wines. The service is excellent and the meals are well prepared. A German chef will soon be arriving to take charge of evening meals and functions. Reservations are essential, even for guests staying at the hotel. If you specify a vegetarian meal when booking, special arrangements will be made with the chef on duty, and an assorted vegetarian menu will be offered to you.

Travellers who would rather eat with the locals should try the cheap and tasty meals at the Qacha's Nek Restaurant, near the Qacha's Nek Shell Filling Station. The menu includes both traditional meals of porridge and mutton or chicken, and more "Western" foods such as fried chips and Russian sausages. This restaurant is popular with the locals.

About 20 m east of the Qacha's Nek Restaurant is the Sea Point Café on the opposite side of the road. Light traditional meals are offered, and more beer is sold than food. It's difficult to find sitting room in the Sea Point, and most customers sit outside to eat their meals.

At the bus and minibus taxi terminal is the Vuku Zenzele Café and Restaurant. With a definite outlaw crowd lurking in the shadows, eating here is an experience fraught with imaginary fears. The meal servings are large and the food is tasty. Try the lamb stew with vegetables and brown bread, helped along with some of the local sorghum brew.

Around the public transport depot are a number of street vendors who sell freshly baked bread, chicken curry and fruit.

In the modern section of Qacha's Nek, travellers will find light fast-food style meals at Nkeletseng Café near Pep Stores and the Cat shop, which also sells biscuits, fruit and crisps. Further into the suburbs are restaurants serving the local population. These are the best places for meeting the hill-men who have brought stock down from the mountains. It is in these hidden eating houses, where few visitors ever venture, that you can put a few more pieces of the Lesotho jigsaw into place.

Things to buy

Although Qacha's Nek has no touristy curio shops, visitors will find a number of places to buy traditional Basotho goods. The Raohang Banna/Basali Association has one of the larger selections available. There is no "official" shop open to the public, but most of the men and women sell craft items. The Association is located a few metres beyond the large market gardens, at the U-shaped bend in the road. Speak to any of the people working in the gardens. Word spreads quickly that a visitor wants to buy something. You will be shown colourful jerseys and shawls, large blankets, wooden carvings depicting traditional Basotho activities, pottery jars and cooking pots. Prices are negotiable, and for the handmade blankets you can expect to pay a fairly high price.

Many of the shops in both sections of Qacha's Nek sell blankets, jerseys and small tapestries. Visitors should wander through the business districts and look in the fabric shops, and even try the Vuku Zenzele Café.

This is the end of the southern route for many visitors. To leave Lesotho from Qacha's Nek, travellers must take the gravel road south-east of the circle, and continue up the road to the border post at the top of the hill. From here it is a short trip into the Transkei, then on to South Africa. Given the political instability in the Transkei, visitors using this route should make enquiries at the RLMP (police) in Qacha's Nek before committing themselves to travelling through the Transkei.

Other visitors may decide to travel further north, either to Sehlabathebe National Park or to Thaba Tseka. Both destinations are challenging, but immensely rewarding. Leave Qacha's Nek, going west, along the A15 national road. About 11 km west of Qacha's Nek is the village of Mpiti. At the road sign pointing the way to Sekake or Qacha's Nek, turn right. At night the turnoff may be difficult to see, but look for the motor workshop at the junction of the two roads. This is a poor gravel road which follows steep contours until levelling off near the village of Tsoelike. From this village the way further north to Thaba Tseka is only accessible to hikers equipped with their own tents, food and maps. Those travellers attempting this strenuous but magnificent route should cross the Tsoelike river on the suspension bridge, and then continue along what is supposed to be the A4 national road. There are no vehicles on this route and hikers will have to walk through uninhabited areas for about 50 km, until reaching the motorable road at Matebeng. Getting a ride to Thaba Tseka from Matebeng depends on the weather, but most travellers arrive in Thaba Tseka within a day.

For people with their own transport or using public transport the only route open is along the B33 road to Sehlabathebe National Park, about 78 km north-east. The drive is through beautiful mountain scenery. At the village of Hill Top, 19 km from Tsoelike, is a view-point high above the Tsoelike river. And near the settlement of Moshebi, 11 km from Sehlabathebe, is the best view-point on the route. From here visitors can look down into South Africa. The British writer, Geoff Combes, claims in his underground travel magazine, *World's Wild Places*, that this view is one of the most spectacular in the world.

SEHLABATHEBE NATIONAL PARK (medium tariff)

With an average altitude of 2 400 m, this park is one of the highest and remotest in Africa. Proclaimed a national park in 1970, this conservation area covers 7 500 ha of mountains, valleys and waterfalls, and is the catchment for the trout-filled upper Tsoelike river. The park offers visitors the chance to see the rare bearded vulture (also known as the lammergeier). Travellers who are prepared to walk the distance can see the tiny Oreodaimonqathlambae fish, thought for decades to be extinct and only recently rediscovered in the lakes of the Drakensberg mountains. Other game that can be seen includes black eagles, baboons, rhebok, eland and occasionally the secretive oribi.

There is no fuel available at Sehlabathebe and travellers with mechanised transport will have to bring enough extra fuel to take them back either to Qacha's Nek, 105 km to the south-west, or the difficult and dangerous 122 km to Thaba Tseka in the north-west. The same goes for food. There are virtually no shops in the area, and the few trading stores only carry the most basic supplies.

Accommodation is available in the Mountain Lodge, at a small hostel or camping. Reservations are said to be essential for all three forms of accommodation, but a glance through the Visitors' Book denies this: travellers arriving without prior booking are accommodated anyway. The lodge has space for 12 visitors in simple rooms, and provides all bedding, ablution facilities and the use of an equipped kitchen. The hostel has beds for six people, water and cooking facilities. If you have a sleeping bag, and the hostel is full (very rare), you will be given a foam mattress and allowed to sleep on the floor.

Camping is allowed anywhere in the park, but you must get a permit from the reception desk at the park office. Campers should remember that it gets bitterly cold in the park, and it is quite common for snow to fall even in midsummer. There are storms all year, and with the Drakensberg mountains being notorious for attracting the most lightning strikes to earth in the world, campers should be cautious in their choice of campsite and take into account the distance from the main camp in case of emergency.

All fees must be paid in cash, and a deposit is required. If you cannot pay in cash, your vehicle will be impounded and you will be kept under house-arrest until the RLMP (police) arrive. Of course you could always try to evade the law by hiking out through the mountains into South Africa. According to the Senior Warden, this is something South African hikers frequently do.

Address: Sehlabathebe Reservations (specify lodge or hostel), Lesotho National Park, Ministry of Agriculture, P.O. Box 92, Maseru, 100, Lesotho
Telephone: (09266) 323600 or 322876

There are three routes out of Sehlabathebe National Park. Travellers with transport can either return to Qacha's Nek, or tackle the scenic drive along the B32 mountain track, up over the Matebeng Pass (2 940 m), down to the village of the same name, and then north for about 82 km to Thaba Tseka.

For those with bicycles or on foot, the most interesting way out is across the mountains into South Africa. You will spend about three days crossing the 24 km to the Lesotho border at Nkonkoana Gate, then go down the bridle path to the South African border post at Bushman's Nek.

This is the end of the Lesotho routes. They will have been as much journeys through the hills and valleys of your soul as through the wilderness areas of the country. The people, like many mountain dwellers at home in a magnificence that dwarfs all human pretension, are humorous and fundamentally realists. It is impossible not to be taught something by them. Their simplicity is not crude; their hospitality is never intrusive; they know when to leave you alone. Dignified themselves, they treat everyone else with dignity. Money and tourism can change many things; all travellers should pray that the quiet decency of the people and the awesome natural beauty will remain unaffected. Honour these remote regions, and if you do, even the simplest and most ordinary experience along the way will shine forever in your memory.

7 HIKING

One of Lesotho's greatest attractions is hiking. Because most of the country is an unfenced wilderness, it offers wonderful walking opportunities. Still relatively unexplored, the mountains and valleys of Lesotho are one of the last destinations for adventure hikers. No doubt this will soon change, and already the government is planning hiking trails for tourists. With the traditional hiking destinations, such as Nepal and Peru, getting overcrowded, hikers will soon start looking to countries like Lesotho and Rwanda. At present, visitors hiking in Lesotho are still unlikely to encounter other hikers.

The most commonly hiked route is the Top-of-the-Berg trail from Sehlabathebe National Park to the Sani Pass border post. It is possible to hike anywhere around the country, and with planning and a sense of adventure, hiking in Lesotho can be a rewarding experience.

The highest mountains in southern Africa are spectacular and unforgettable. Hikers will have the chance of becoming one with the wilderness. There is a wide variety of birds, flowers and small creatures to be seen, so take along a bird identification guide, animal and wildflower books and a butterfly guide – butterflies fill the mountain meadows in summer and autumn.

The crime rate is low, and hikers need not worry about being robbed or attacked. It makes good sense though not to hike alone; the ideal is two people. You can expect to pass isolated villages where children of up to 10 years old have never seen foreigners, and to sleep in the stone huts of shepherds high on the ridges of mountains. The differences in lifestyle between mountain and lowland clans will become obvious, and you may find yourself beginning to understand the reasons behind the disharmony that affects much of tribal Africa.

Hikers will find the Basotho a happy, friendly and hospitable people. Expect to be invited to spend a night or share a meal in villages along the way. The culture of the Basotho demands assistance to travellers, and it is to the benefit of all tourists who follow you that you are sensitive to offers from the locals. If you find yourself outdoors at night and needing shelter, approach a village to ask for assistance.

Prepare thoroughly before you set off to hike in Lesotho. It is vital that you be fit and healthy; the weather, terrain and physical demands of trekking through the highest country on the African continent should be carefully considered and planned for. Get a copy of the Lesotho topographical map from the Department of Surveys in Maseru (P.O. Box 876, Maseru, 100). Plan a trip that is within your physical abilities. There are hikes that can take just four hours (such as to the summit of Makholo), and hikes that last at least five days (to explore the central wilderness of the country). For visitors arriving from lowland or coastal areas, it is better to start your hike in the lower regions of the country and gradually acclimatise yourself to the altitude. All hiking will be above 1 500 m and can even be above 3 400 m. The air is rarefied and cold – something that needs to be considered when it comes to selecting cooking facilities and clothing.

A typical hike in one day covers a number of ascents and descents (there is very little level land in Lesotho), and should last four to six hours. Start out early and make camp before nightfall, giving yourself enough time to prepare dinner and relax. For a special treat, bargain for some goat or ewe milk from local shepherds. The rich creamy milk is delicious in coffee or with breakfast. Keeping the milk fresh is not a problem and winter hikers may even wake up to find the milk frozen.

Although winter is bitterly cold with frequent snowfalls, it is the best time to go hiking in Lesotho. Because of high rainfall and severe storms in summer, hiking from October to February can be unpleasant. In winter the early mornings are very cold, but as soon as the sun rises so does the temperature. The air is clear, visibility is excellent and most hikers are invigorated and eager to begin walking. Snowstorms obviously pose a problem, and all winter hikers should have adequate clothing and provisions when venturing up into the uninhabited areas of Lesotho.

Hikers visiting Lesotho in summer should pack rain-gear. The advantage of summer hiking is the abundance of wild flowers and the chance to meet the hillmen who tend their flocks above 2 500 m. Beware though of the sudden mists which often descend during late summer, making the cliffs slippery and dangerous. There are numerous caves in the mountains of Lesotho, and in summer they provide a comfortable if somewhat eerie place to spend the night.

All your hiking and camping equipment must be brought into the country, because equipment is limited, expensive and impossible to hire in Lesotho. Some gear can be borrowed from lodges, but only for day hikes. Take along a good quality backpack (with side pouches), a down-filled mummy-style sleeping bag, a warm jacket and corduroy trousers, worn-in hiking boots, cooking facilities and extra clothing. Even food should be brought in. After a few days of eating the local mutton and porridge, it makes a pleasant change to eat some differently flavoured food. For daytime snacks, take along fruit and nuts and glucose sweets.

The rivers of Lesotho are bilharzia free, but are often contaminated through washing and toilet use. Carry your own water bottle and some method of purifying drinking water.

Possibly the best way of showing your gratitude for shelter or food is by giving your host a box of matches or a pen, or sharing some of your own food. Hard currency is not always appreciated, especially in the remote villages where bartering takes preference over cash. One South African hiker found that cheap cigarette lighters were always appreciated.

Organised hiking is still virtually non-existent, and hikers must do most things themselves. On the shorter walks, guides can often be arranged. Contact the manager of the lodge or hotel nearest to your destination and ask for a local guide. The staff at the Leribe Hotel and Sani Top Chalet are particularly good. The fee is negligible, but hikers are expected to supply the guide with food along the trail. Porters are not available, and you will be required to carry your own equipment. An alternative is to hire a donkey or mule to carry the gear.

COMMON TREKS

Thabana Ntlenyana summit (3 482 m)

This hike takes about eight hours and is fairly demanding. There is no need for specialised equipment, and a day-pack with extra jersey and some food will be sufficient. The two popular routes to the mountain are either from the Sani Top border, or across the hills from the Kotisephola Pass (3 240 m). If you are leaving from the Sani Top Chalet, a guide and donkey can be arranged for the trip. From the Kotisephola Pass, hikers will have to make their own way to the summit. The views from the summit of the highest mountain in southern Africa are truly spectacular. The trail up from the Sani Top Chalet can be busy over weekends, and it is better to make the trip during the week.

Lebihan/Maletsunyane Falls

These are the highest single-drop falls in southern Africa, plummeting nearly 200 m into a dark pool below. The walk is a round trip of about 8 km from Semonkong and usually takes about six hours including the time spent at the falls. Accommodation is not a problem as there are two tourist lodges near the falls. Guides can be arranged from either of the lodges, but visitors are advised to negotiate the price with the lodge manager rather than guide.

Semonkong to Nkua

This route traverses some of the remotest areas of Lesotho and passes through uninhabited regions. It usually takes about three days to cover the 30 km. Guides are not available and an ability to use a compass and read a topographical map is an advantage. From Semonkong go west to St Leonard's Mission. Turn right onto the gravel road, walk past two traditional villages and then take the second track to the right, which swings south-east towards Nkau. You will be required to carry all your food and camping requirements. Take water in bottles, as most of the route is along the crests of hills with the only water down in the steep-sided valleys.

Top-of-the-Berg

Most hikers start this route from the Sehlabathebe National Park at the Nkonkoana Gate border with South Africa. This is a truly spectacular hike along the edge of the Drakensberg escarpment. The trail ends, after about four days, at Sani Pass. It is strenuous and visitors who are unfit should not attempt this hike. The weather is unpredictable and during summer there are violent afternoon thunderstorms. When hiking in autumn and summer, walkers often encounter other hikers. Unlike other routes through Lesotho, the Top-of-the-Berg trail is well used. It offers a challenging route along the highest ridges in Lesotho, early mornings when cloud fills the valleys of South Africa, and a liberating sensation of freedom up on the peaks. Come prepared with tent, warm clothing, food and water, down-filled sleeping bag and topographical map. With plunging cliffs marking at least one side of the path, hikers must keep together and be careful when walking in the rain or at night. At Sani Top there is a mountaineer's chalet with hot showers, bedding and a well stocked bar.

8 PONY-TREKKING

Ponies have for decades been the traditional Basotho transport. Living in a mountainous country the Basotho have bred ponies that are sure-footed, agile and even-tempered. Pony-treks take visitors away from busy national roads and towns, into the hills and valleys that are the real Lesotho. Pony-trekking in Lesotho has become a major tourist attraction, and although it is expensive, no visit to Lesotho is complete without a riding excursion. For many visitors a pony-trek remains the highlight of their Lesotho journey, and people often return for longer, more adventurous treks.

The main centre for pony-trekking is the Basotho Pony Project, 60 km from Maseru near the Molimo-Nthuse Lodge. From Maseru take the A3 east and turn left onto the mountain road for Thaba Tseka. About 8 km from Bushman's Pass (2 226 m), on the left side of the gravel road, is the entrance to the Basotho Pony Project. To get there from Thaba Tseka, travel west along the A3 national road, past Mantsonyane and up the Blue Mountain Pass (2 626 m). About 5 km further, on the right of the road, is the Project. Travellers using public transport should ask the driver to drop them off at the "Ponies".

The busiest period at the Project is during summer and autumn (October–April), and visitors who intend riding should book well in advance; at least a month, according to the manager. No previous experience is necessary and the guides are adept at judging which pony to assign to individuals – some guides have been on training courses in Tourism and spent time attending classes in Ireland. Pony-trekkers are expected to bring their own sleeping bags, camping gear, food and clothing, including a hat. Remember that even during summer Lesotho can be cold. Take sufficient warm clothing and wet-weather gear. Although this is not a prerequisite, it is a good idea to get fit before attempting one of the longer rides.

Several treks are available, ranging from one hour to seven days. Visitors are often disappointed when they arrive at the Project only to find that the trek has been cancelled because of poor weather – phone the day before you are due to leave. The longer routes are only available if there are sufficient riders, but the manager is willing to negotiate a few days' trek for individuals.

No accommodation is available at the Basotho Pony Project and most visitors either stay at the Molimo-Nthuse Lodge 2 km away, or arrange transport from the Hotel Victoria in Maseru. This hotel has a courtesy bus that may also be used by non-guests for a fee. People who arrive with tents or vehicles in which they can sleep are allowed to camp at the Pony Project. No fee is charged, and it is a beautiful place at which to spend a night.

Tours available include:

- A short one-hour ride in the immediate area around the Basotho Pony Project. This tour provides hardly enough time to get a real feel for the adventure of pony-trekking.
- To Leboela Falls. This trek lasts about two hours and goes through some interesting villages and spectacular countryside.
- A trip to the Qiloane Falls 8 km away, which passes through magnificent valleys sculpted by the Makhaleng river. According to the manager of the Basotho Pony Project, this is the best tour for getting an introduction to pony-trekking in Lesotho.
- Two days and one night away is the most popular trek; suitable over a weekend for visitors who must return to work on Monday. This trek passes through traditional villages, up onto high mountain ridges and alongside fast-flowing streams.
- For parties of not less than two, the trek of two nights and three days takes riders far off the main roads. You will sleep in villages and eat with the locals. Once over the saddle-ache of the first day, pony-trekkers will begin to feel comfortable in the saddle and be able to relax and enjoy the stimulating scenery.
- A good trek for visitors who have had some previous experience is over four nights and five days. Once again you will be accommodated in stone and thatch huts and be able to live, for a while, with the tribal people of Lesotho.
- If you are crazy enough to want a longer ride, and mean to lose yourself completely in the adventure of Lesotho, then the trek of six nights, seven days is the one to choose. Going in a southerly direction to Semonkong and the Lebihan Falls, the route takes in some of the finest scenery in the country. In spite of the length of this trek, visitors who have tried it always rave about it. Part of the fascination of the trek is being able to meet the medicine men in some of the remote villages. Usually old, they live a life that is not really of earth, and visitors often emerge from the encounter with a different attitude to

life. There is no rush on the tour and apart from looking at the awesome scenery, there is little else to do but relax and drift into the timelessness of Lesotho's splendour.

Address: Basotho Pony Project, P.O. Box 1027, Maseru, 100, Lesotho
Telephone: (09266) 314165

Another pony-trekking centre is the Matelile Pony Owners' Association, located near the Malealea Lodge, about 84 km south of Maseru on the B401. From Maseru follow the signs to Mafeteng along the A2 national road. About 10 km south of Morija turn left onto the B40 road. Follow the right fork in the road to where the B401 turns left to Malealea. Flights to Malealea can also be taken from Moshoeshoe International Airport near Maseru. Hitching or using public transport from Maseru to Malealea involves a few difficulties. To find a bus or minibus taxi heading south, go to the new bus depot about 1,5 km south of Cathedral Circle in Maseru, along the Main South 1 road. Take a bus going to Mafeteng and ask to be dropped off at the turning to Malealea on the B40. From here you will either have to hitch the rest of the way, or try to flag down one of the minibus taxis that travel the route.

Not government controlled, as is the Basotho Pony Project, this pony-trekking outfit is owned by the locals. They hire their ponies out to riders and the fee for each pony goes to its owner, after a small percentage has been kept for administration purposes. This pony-trekking centre lacks the financial backing of the Lesotho and Irish governments, which the Basotho Pony Project has, and is best suited to those travellers who can endure some degree of hardship.

Trips offered by the Matelile Pony Owners' Association include:

- An introductory ride of about four hours to the Bots'oela Falls. This trek can be taken throughout the year and includes stops at well-preserved Bushman paintings. In summer visitors can swim in the icy mountain pools and rivers.
- A trek of one night and two days to the Ribaneng Falls takes riders into the heart of this wild region. Not an easy trip, it catapults riders into the way of life of the pony-riding tribesmen of the hills.
- Perhaps the most exciting of the pony-treks offered is the one that goes to three of the country's most stunning waterfalls: Lebihan, Ketane and Ribaneng Falls. Lasting three nights and four days, this trek includes side-trips to Bushman paintings in mysterious hidden caves. Visitors sleep in well-maintained village huts, swim in isolated rock pools and meet the quiet shepherds who occasionally stop to

greet the riders. For those who enjoy the outdoors with all its beauty and unpredictability, this is definitely the pony-trek to take.

Reservations are advisable, but visitors who want to ride in winter or spring can usually just turn up a few days before a scheduled trip. Once again, pony-treks are dependent on weather conditions, and there is no guarantee that a trek will take place on a specific date. Tours and guides are best reserved through the efficient and capable management of the Malealea Lodge.

Address: Malealea Lodge, Pony-treks, P.O. Box Makhakhe, 922, Lesotho, or P.O. Box 119, Wepener 9944, South Africa
Telephone: (09266) 785336 or 785264
Fax: 785326

Reservations for both pony-trekking centres can also be made through the Tourist Board, P.O. Box 1378, Maseru, 100, Lesotho; tel. (09266) 322896, fax 310108, telex 4280 LO.

APPENDIX: USEFUL ADDRESSES

Customs and Immigration (visas, limits and extensions)
Director of Immigration and Passport Services, P.O. Box 363, Maseru, 100, Lesotho
Telephone: (09266) 322187

Ministry of Agriculture (domestic animals, avian and fish species)
Director of Quarantine Services, P.O. Box 24, Maseru, 100, Lesotho
Telephone: (09266) 324843

Director of Fisheries (fishing permits)
P.O. Box 24, Maseru, 100, Lesotho
Telephone: (09266) 323986

Historical Protection and Preservation Commission (permits for archaeological digs, exploration and fossil hunting)
The Permanent Secretary, P.O. Box 1125, Maseru, 100, Lesotho
Telephone: (09266) 322705

Civil Aviation Department (flight plans, weather reports, clearances and permits)
The Director, P.O. Box 629, Maseru, 100, Lesotho
Telephone: (09266) 322499

Department of Police (matters relating to law and order)
Royal Lesotho Mounted Police Headquarters, P.O. Box 13, Maseru, 100, Lesotho
Telephone: (09266) 323061

District Administration (information on remote areas)
The Secretary, P.O. Box 28, Maseru, 100, Lesotho
Telephone: (09266) 325047

Ministry of Health (information on medical services in specific regions)
The Director, P.O. Box 514, Maseru, 100, Lesotho
Telephone: (09266) 324404

Ministry of Information (press cards, pamphlets and government news)
Principal Secretary, P.O. Box 36, Maseru, 100, Lesotho
Telephone: (09266) 323561

Ministry of Tourism, Sport and Culture (tourist information)
Deputy Principal Secretary, P.O. Box 52, Maseru, 100, Lesotho
Telephone: (09266) 313034

Ministry of Transport (public transport routes, details on road conditions and motoring advice)
The Director, P.O. Box 413, Maseru, 100, Lesotho
Telephone: (09266) 323691

INDEX

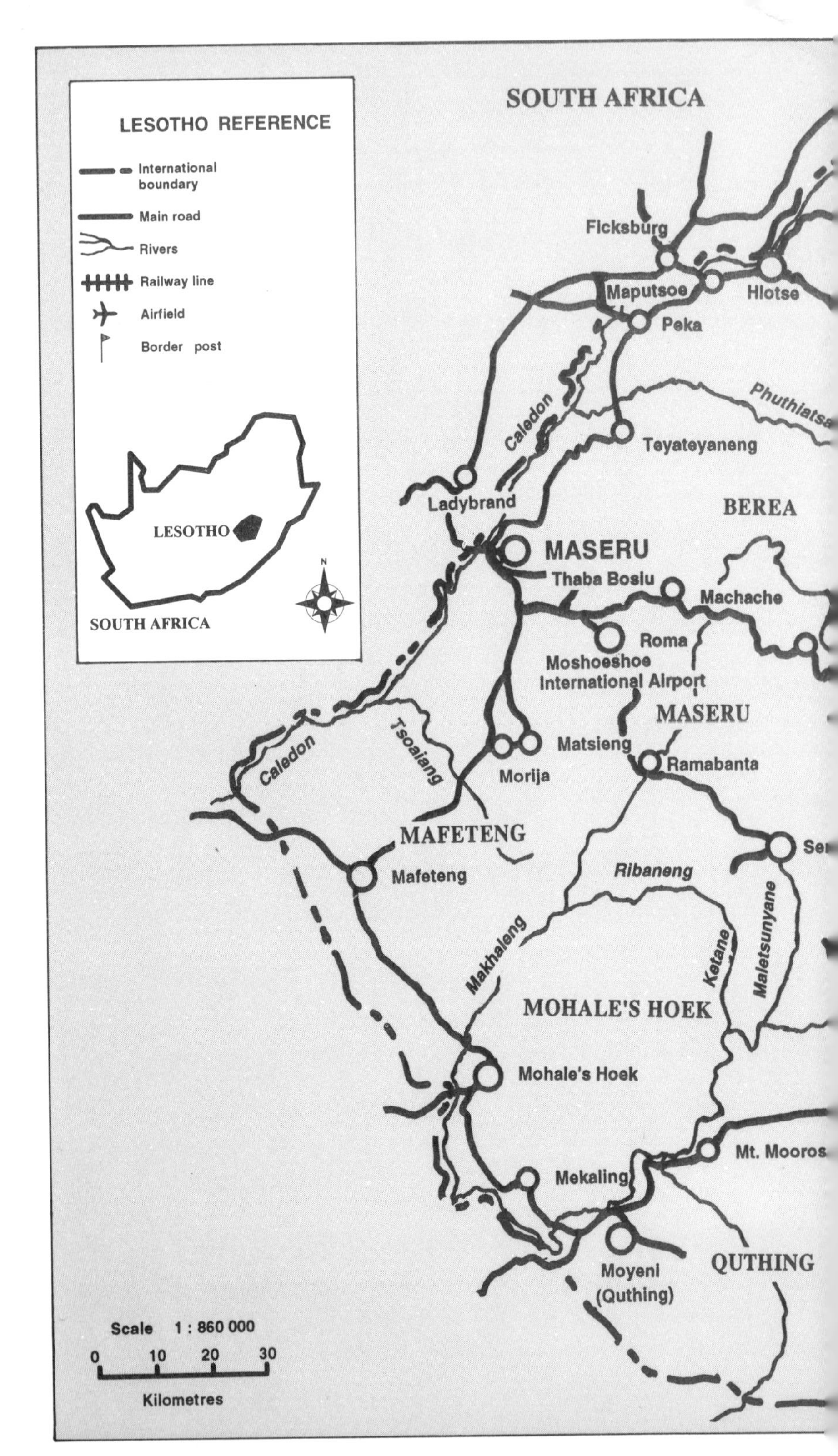

LESOTHO REFERENCE
International boundary
Main road
Rivers
Railway line
Airfield
Border post
LESOTHO
SOUTH AFRICA
N
SOUTH AFRICA
Ficksburg
Maputsoe
Hlotse
Peka
Phuthiatsa
Caledon
Teyateyaneng
Ladybrand
BEREA
MASERU
Thaba Bosiu
Machache
Roma
Moshoeshoe International Airport
MASERU
Matsieng
Ramabanta
Tsoaiang
Caledon
Morija
MAFETENG
Mafeteng
Ribaneng
Ketane
Maletsunyane
Makhaleng
MOHALE'S HOEK
Mohale's Hoek
Mt. Mooros
Mekaling
Moyeni (Quthing)
QUTHING
Scale 1 : 860 000
0 10 20 30
Kilometres